Centerville Library
Washington-Centerville Public Library
DISCARD
Centerville, Ohio

MAKING BOLD MOVES

Creating Multimillion-Dollar Success in 500 Days or Less!

D1270616

William S. Parrish, Jr.

Foreword by Derek T. Dingle,
Editor-In-Chief, Black Enterprise

MBM Publishing

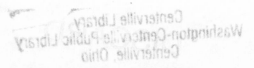
Centerville Library
Washington-Centerville Public Library
Centerville, Ohio

Copyright © **2011** William S. Parrish, Jr.
All rights reserved. No part of this book may be reproduced in any way or by any means, including electronic, mechanical, photocopying or otherwise, without the proper written permission and consent of the publisher.

Making Bold Moves
Creating Multimillion Dollar Success in 500 Days or Less!

Written by William S. Parrish, Jr.
President & CEO - NobleStrategy, LLC

Foreword by Derek T. Dingle
Editor-in-Chief, Black Enterprise

Artwork & Cover Design by Jorge Naranjo
Photo by Hassan Kinley

Published in the United States of America
MBM Publishing, LLC
www.makingboldmovesnow.com

Printed in the United States of America
ISBN # 978-0983906803
ISBN# 0983906807

DEDICATION

This book is dedicated to the family, friends and colleagues who have shaped my experiences and perspective along my journey from high school to Hampton University and beyond; who supported my early entrepreneurial vision, allowed me to make bold moves and reach my version of success, and teach others along the way ...

And with Manhood, Perseverance, Scholarship and Uplift this book is dedicated to all of my Brothers of the Omega Psi Phi Fraternity, Inc. ...

And for my creator who strengthens me, I thank my Lord and Savior Jesus Christ!

TABLE OF CONTENTS

ACKNOWLEDGEMENTS

I am sincerely grateful for the tangible and intangible assistance received in completing this first in a series of books. The resources, prayers, words of encouragement and actions afforded me during my two-year writing and editing process have served me well. I am thankful to my mentors who helped guide my decision making and the employees who helped build my vision over the last six years.

To the first class of employees who trusted me when all we had was a vision and a shared second floor office suite, I want to again say thank you. To my sister Jennifer Darschel who served as my first all-everything—from assistant to operations manager, successfully holding down the fort while I traveled to and from New York to drum up business—I sincerely appreciate you and the work you have done. I am also very thankful for my editor and copyeditor on this book, Tawana Bivins Rosenbaum and Sonja Mack, who pushed me to read, re-read and revise in order to tell the best story I could.

I am most grateful to my mother, Roberta Daisy Parrish, who always told me I could do anything if I applied myself. Mom, in the beginning I didn't exactly know what you meant but I quickly learned. To my dad, William Samuel Parrish, Sr. for offering your support in your own way, showing me what to do and what not to do, and how hard work always pays off, I am thankful to have learned those lessons that surely made me a better man. I am extremely grateful for my two loving children, Khari Osei and Alieke Ajoia, for whom I have worked tirelessly to provide instruction and examples. You both have given me the determination to work harder in my business and the pleasure of working even harder to be the best dad I can be for you.

Lastly, I cannot give enough thanks to warrant all the love and support my lovely wife, Dr. Jennifer Payne Parrish, has shown me but I will still try. Jennifer, you are truly an inspiration to me and a phenomenal woman. I am blessed to have you in my life and know I am that much better because of you. I cherish our marriage and friendship and look forward to growing our relationship even further together during the rest of our lives.

FOREWORD

When Bill Parrish asked me to contribute the foreword for this book, I was both honored and excited. Over the past few years, I have found Bill to represent the type of innovative entrepreneur that we often chronicle in the pages of BLACK ENTERPRISE. In building NobleStrategy, he not only built a force in the construction management industry, he built one of the few black-owned companies that have become a leader in the $90 billion-dollar green economy—one of the sectors that President Obama has encouraged companies, large and small, to enter in order to out-innovate and out-compete the rest of the world.

At BLACK ENTERPRISE, we have always had high regard for Bill's acumen as an entrepreneur and his reputation as an innovator. His company has been a nominee for one of our Small Business of the Year awards and he has served as a panelist on sessions at our events, including a session I moderated at our 2011 Black Enterprise Entrepreneurs Conference on how small businesses can take advantage of the rapidly growing green space—from gaining LEED certification in order to access government contracts to becoming more profitable through greater energy efficiency.

Developing strategies to earn more green in the green arena is but one area that Bill covers in this book. When I read it, I thought it was a powerful, valuable resource for both emerging and established business owners written by a visionary, relentless entrepreneur.

The lessons you can learn in this book come at an apt time. As the black jobless rate stands at 16%, legions of African Americans will have to embrace entrepreneurship as a means of finding employment and wealth building opportunities. To make a further impact on the unemployment situation, African Americans must develop lasting commercial institutions. According to SBA Deputy Administrator Marie Johns, of the 2 million or so black-owned businesses nationwide, 95% are represented by self-employed individuals. And as you would expect, a recent American Express OPEN survey revealed that the greatest concern for small businesses and would-be entrepreneurs is cash flow: 66% were concerned about whether they had sufficient resources to keep their firms buoyant. Recent statistics also show an economy that is becoming increasingly sluggish and that has grown less than 1% in the first half of 2011.

Intrepid, passionate and tenacious, Bill believes that one cannot and should not use such macro and micro challenges as excuses to "throw in the towel" or, worse yet, not even get in the game. I encourage you to open the pages of this book to discover how you can thrive as a business owner in today's uncertain times by developing essential management, marketing, sales and opportunity-spotting skills.

If you want to gain insight into the lives of entrepreneurs and what it truly takes to succeed then this book is for you.

Derek T. Dingle
Editor-in-Chief, BLACK ENTERPRISE

INTRODUCTION

In order to gain the most from *Making Bold Moves: Creating Multimillion-Dollar Success in 500 Days or Less!,* it is important that you understand why I wrote it and the time, place, and circumstances that led to NobleStrategy's relatively quick success in the very competitive New York City construction market. With the financial market meltdown, rising unemployment, and failing businesses, the period from late 2006 through the end of 2010 proved to be severely damaging to the U.S. and world economies. Add in several major world disasters and catastrophes—major earthquakes in Haiti, China, Chile, Tibet and Japan; cyclones in Myanmar; and major flooding in Pakistan and the United States— and there is no wonder why communities across the globe are suffering and the recession continues to erode international currencies. So how was it that an emerging firm could start and grow exponentially amidst so many difficulties and severe market conditions? This is my story. And although I prepared for as much as I could, I was not ready for what was coming.

If timing is everything, why start a business during rough times? Perhaps it would have been better to wait until the economy improved or to hold off until the financing returned, but I was ready to get it done and make it happen! It was truly an uphill battle trying to create a winning plan that would attract key public agency clients to a start-up firm without a recognized name or reputation. It was also extremely difficult, as a new firm, to find a fit in the marketplace, where we would be considered valuable enough to complement large project teams. We took on the mission of being a professional construction resource seeking to add value to existing projects and larger firms. We succeeded in our mission but not first without making major sacrifices, which included working without pay, extending personal guarantees, foregoing family health coverage, and adapting to a 24/7 business mentality where you're never really off from work. Not quite the picture I thought entrepreneurship would be—me lying in a hammock on the beach and multitasking from my BlackBerry. It always looked so nice in the business magazines, but starting out, that type of freedom just didn't exist. If that is also your image of entrepreneurship or business success, I'd like to create for you another version of what business success really looks like across these pages.

Although I'm able to share my experiences, even as they continue to unfold, about business success, I am by no means on easy street. Our company is still responding to business challenges every day. I still work an average of 50 to 60 hours a week, and sometimes I don't see enough cash flow to pay myself first, which is a cardinal rule. I don't have an unusually high net worth yet and have not achieved private jet fractional ownership, which is on my to-do list, so I still fly coach. I maintain enough debt to stay motivated but I also maintain enough credit to do good business. My truck is eight years old with over 150,000 miles on it but I am still *making bold moves* and achieving business success.

Though it may not seem very glamorous, I still wake up every day to enjoy doing what I love. I still get to be my own boss and build a profitable business while leaving a legacy for a community of entrepreneurs in the next generation. I still get to create jobs and add balance to that never-ending argument of not being able to find qualified professionals in this field. (Most folks just don't know where to look.) I am enjoying the fruits of my labor and creating my own version of business success, which is fulfilling at work, at home and in my community. People will benefit from the work that I do, and I will be richer for my giving as long as I can get you to the next level, which is part of the reason I am telling my story now. How else would my next story about how we achieved $100 million in revenue mean anything if you didn't know where we started from and what it looked like in the beginning, when we were only at $3 million in sales—which was still pretty far from my goal, albeit a major accomplishment.

As you read you will also benefit from knowing my true motivation for telling my story and why I felt compelled to share the most intimate details. I believe that if I can help you win then I win, too. No matter what the game, if I become a resource that you can trust, then you will eventually seek me out. No amount of marketing can surpass what satisfied clients and word-of-mouth referrals can do for a growing organization or a trusted expert authority on a particular subject.

If it happened for me it can happen for you, so I take great pride in telling my story to those who can grow from it. For years I practiced coaching firms as an employee and was always focused on building capacity in emerging firms. But after years of management and advocacy as an agency owner, then starting and growing a minority-owned business during a recession, I knew there were valuable lessons I'd learned that I could share with you that would get you to business success. I used to think that in order to write a book that would be helpful to people, you first had to reach some very high pinnacle of success. But I actually got the idea to write this book much earlier than that. While I did reach a relative pinnacle of success—achieving sales of $1.7 million about 500 days from our start and having piloted a start-up through a difficult and competitive marketplace to take an industry position as a leader and well-sought out firm—we knew we could do more before our story would be complete. Even when we reached revenues of $3 million just a few short years later, initially, I was not convinced that our story would be relevant before we reached our peak.

However, what struck me was the value in the journey, not the destination. As I watched the U.S. financial and world disasters wreck the economy, I continued to consume more and more of the business biographies of folks who were very successful. I noticed that they discussed their victories but also always seemed to share disappointments and failures as part of their stories. That led me to realize that it is not so much the level of success you achieve but what you experience along the way that becomes the best element of your story. The jewels of knowledge that are cloaked in the accounts and experiences that the entrepreneur has soaked in and been stretched by—accounts and experiences that I have certainly had my share of—begin to shape the opinions and perspective of savvy business leaders who can be guided by inner wisdom and business acumen. The more difficult and, sometimes, disastrous the experience, the sharper your perspective and market intuition becomes, which inevitably helps you grow.

If you've heard the adage "Nothing ventured, nothing gained," then you can understand how not having been exposed to any crisis could stunt your growth in certain areas. That is why leading job candidates with specialized training and high levels of education sometimes lose out to more seasoned, experienced professionals. If you have never lived through and found your way out of disastrous scenarios, who would want to depend on you to pull them through that which will surely come? Whether in business, life, sports, politics, or even in the family dynamic, you often get rewarded for the difficult situations you have been able to steer clear of or the tragedies you have presided over with ease.

We have seen how political careers have been launched based on how folks responded during a crisis and we have also seen how star athletes get rewarded with lucrative contracts because they have been on championship teams. Simply put, experience is valuable. And in business, before you make the same mistakes, reduce your risk and learn from the mistakes and successes of others, including me.

It took me a while but, at some point, I realized the appeal of my expertise, mistakes, and small victories that brought me knowledge and growth and could be used to actually motivate and inspire business owners. That's when I knew I had to find a way to record my experiences and organize my thoughts for an effective how-to example, which resulted in many business seminars, contributed magazine columns, conference speeches, university lectures, postings on social media platforms and now this book!

This book is actually written as a series of discussions, where each chapter provides guidance in mastering one of 14 very effective rules for quickly ramping up and engaging your market for immediate success in about a year and a half, which is what we did. Each chapter also contains my story, including real issues with clients, competitors, owners, alliance partners and family, which can assist you in building an advantage within your industry for immediate success.

We have accomplished a lot in a short period of time, and by no means are we finished. One of my short-term goals is to profitably achieve $100 million in sales by 2015, which would mark our 10th year of major operations. But one of my immediate, more important goals is to be able to bonus a quarter of a million dollars to my employees for their hard work. The sales figures and lofty revenue projections are fantastic and will keep me focused on my work, but if I can create wealth within my organization with the people who helped me build it from the ground up—that stands out as a far greater legacy than reaching $100 million in sales.

As you read, my hope is that the lessons communicated and the personal reflections on how we actually made it happen during our initial years (2005-2007) and how we have continued that growth (2007-present) will provide a tool kit to assist you in starting, managing, and growing your business. This book will support you by providing a nontraditional recipe that includes details on the following: how and when to make your transition into entrepreneurship *(Chapter 1: Coming to the Stage)*, defining what you really want out of your business *(Chapter 2: Deciding You Want to Win Big)*, preparing for your eventual business and family changes *(Chapter 3: Planning to be Successful)*, how to sustain yourself until your great ideas pay off *(Chapter 4: Getting Paid Now and More Later)*, developing your faith and calculating business decisions *(Chapter 5: Take Risks, Have Faith and Keep Planting Seeds)*, creating the culture that provides solutions that work for your clients and render your competition nonexistent *(Chapter 6: Creating Wins for the Client)*, developing a strategy to sell services to larger firms *(Chapter 7: Pitching the Primes)*, lessons on what matters in working for larger public or private clients *(Chapter 8: Landing the "Big Fish" Client)*, why doing good for others is good for you *(Chapter 9: Community Service for Your Business)*, being a resource to elected officials and assisting them in advocating for your concerns *(Chapter 10: Business Politics)*, using social media and nontraditional means of marketing, advertising and promotions *(Chapter 11: Getting the Word Out)*, the importance of developing a solid environmental business strategy *(Chapter 12: Go Green for More Money and More Market Share)*, how to sustain growth through regular and consistent research, education and practice, away from your clients *(Chapter 13: Be About Practice)*, and a final word on implementing your plan, building your team and getting mentored, personally and professionally *(Chapter 14: What Do We Do Next?)*.

Investing time in mastering these rules will create momentum for you to achieve your wildest dreams of business success. I know it works and it has supported my dreams coming true. Surely, you do have wild dreams about the level of business success you can attain. Then let this book serve as an important motivational reminder that if you are prepared to *Make Bold Moves*, it can and will happen for you, just like it happened for me.

So how big are your dreams, and do you actually believe they can come true? Are you prepared for what life would be like if they did? Could you really just live comfortably with your business success, without a lot of excess, as most people say they could? Or do you want it all? If you answer truthfully, build up your expertise, are willing to follow the rules outlined in this book, and can commit to practicing them as they appear, with faith, then *you* may have a story to tell soon.

I would expect it to be about a year and a half after you've taken the plunge into entrepreneurship or after you've read this book that you would be ... *making bold moves!* I look forward to hearing all about the bold moves you are making and how this book has supported your growth on our blog at **makingboldmovesnow.com**.

CHAPTER 1

COMING TO THE STAGE

In the early 1990s the legendary Apollo Theater was catapulted into mainstream popularity with their television production *It's Showtime at the Apollo*. They introduced to some and presented to others many entertainers and performers with their signature announcement, "Coming to the stage ... !" It didn't always mean the amateur performers would be ready for their nationally televised debut or that the crowd would be ready for them, but they were, no doubt, up next. Did they perfect their act before standing in front of the audience? Were they dressed appropriately to be taken seriously on national television? Did they have the technical precision and expertise to make a smash hit right from the start? Whether or not they had all those things covered, when they heard "*Coming to the stage ... !*" it meant their opportunity had come. And ready or not, they needed to make the best of it.

A start-up business can and should operate in the same manner. Whether launching a new product or creating a new promotion for an established venture, you won't always be able to tell when it's the right time, but when you hear your calling you need to make a move. The moment may not always seem right and sometimes the environment may even create obstacles for your entry into the market. But once you have decided it is your time, you need to *make a bold move* and get started. Get to the stage, in good times or bad times, with your bright ideas and push to create opportunities to make it happen the way you have so often dreamed that it would.

Even in uncertain times you can build a business and be successful. You won't always be able to predict what will occur in the market that will affect your business but you must be ready. Since there is never a "good time" to start your business or push out with your idea, assess your timing, tolerance and the environment and make the best of it with a *bold move*. Get to the stage now! Is the market ready for you? Are you ready for the market? Unless you are willing to put your dreams on hold like most people do, find the courage to start from where you are. *Make a bold move* and get to the stage now! Now is the time that you can win it all—by creating a solid plan, taking action, and making a series of *bold moves* required to gain momentum on your current or planned business. It won't be easy and it won't always look good, but if you can weather the storms that will surely confront you in the early business years, you can come out on top. If you can secure financing, attract talented professionals, and create lasting impressions with clients, then you are trending in the right direction. Do you have a "Coming to the stage" story or moment? I'm sure you do and it lies deep within you. But the challenge is to get it out, so plan on *making bold moves*!

My "Coming to the stage" moment occurs throughout the pages of this book as I recount how our firm got started and offer tips you can use to create your own version of success. I know you can do it because I did it, and I achieved my definition of business success in a very short period of time. As a matter of fact, I will share lessons I learned and applied over a 500-day period—less than a year and a half—that led me to build a new business that grossed approximately $3 million in 2009, in the midst of a depression-era economy. It didn't seem like the best time to quit a job and start a new venture but I did. It didn't seem that I could attract financing to buy my own building in a depressed market but I did. It didn't seem that people would give me a chance and work for me as I followed my dreams but they did. I was *making bold moves*, trying to get to the stage where I could make my own decisions and be the titan in business I had so often read about through other people's stories.

For us, the business is construction management, which many people have never heard of. It's a professional discipline that orchestrates and synthesizes all of the elements of the building process for an owner. Construction managers become the eyes and ears of an owner, who may have money to build a new project but not necessarily the time or expertise to negotiate and manage issues associated with architects, contractors, communities, and building departments on new construction or renovation projects. We manage the building process on commercial projects largely consisting of public sector city and state government entities where construction and development is usually fraught with all kinds of problems, including environmental concerns, land rights, community workforce demands, contractor pricing and evaluation, architect and engineering drawing interpretation, project scheduling, and subcontractor and vendor diversity and utilization, as well as legal contracting dispute resolution. This is *our* business and our firm is called NobleStrategy! We know this business can be tough for owners and that it requires a planned, tactical strategy to execute any project with so many complex issues. We believe if we can think strategically for the benefit of our clients, we can cause them to win with our approach. As long as our approach is true and steadfast, we consider it noble. Once we start with a noble approach, we end up with a noble strategy for the client win! A noble approach ... a NobleStrategy.

Our quick rise to prominence occurred during the worst recession the United States has seen since 1931. With banks failing, businesses closing, and employee layoffs on the rise, we were able to jump into the market, build a successful brand, and make a major contribution to our industry from a virtually unknown status a few years earlier. Facing major corporate collapses and a shrinking economy, and tagged by rising unemployment, President Barack Obama implemented three government-funded stimulus plans to keep major industry and employers afloat. But the planned residual effects didn't exactly trickle down to small business. Nonetheless, we planned to succeed and that's what we reached for. We made some great moves along the way, creating relationships that propelled our firm. But we also made some decisions that did not bear fruit.

One of our worst decisions was pursuing work for a government entity that was really all about politics without really being concerned about what was required to assist with business growth. We made the honest mistake of trying to do our best job for the client and, in the process, ended up offending a favored contractor. I didn't realize it at the time but our pressing attempts to confirm work and contracting commitments wasn't appreciated by those who had the influence at the time. We quickly learned that politics and political favor rule the day and play a very important role in business. We never had the opportunity to grow with the agency and, ultimately, decided not to pursue any more of their work. The good news is, because we were growing but still small, we could quickly change direction and deploy resources in a more efficient manner. Even with the grim financial news that permeated our daily lives from late 2007 through 2010, our firm somehow found a way to prosper and actually grew to record success.

In the first three formal years our business operated, we were able to increase revenue and staff by at least 30% each year from 2006 to 2009. We built a strong brand in an overcrowded market and established a reputation for creative solutions for clients, causing them to win. I was ecstatic when I learned that after six months in operation, we had grossed almost $750K. This was really a confidence builder. We came out of the gate and nearly made three quarters of a million dollars. What a rush! While it may have seemed that we were *always* ready to come to the stage with our brand and solutions, all the conditions were not right for us to start when we did. However, if you wait for perfect conditions, you may never get started. I wasn't going to wait any longer than I had to and grew quite impatient trying to prepare for the right time.

I had formulated a well-crafted extraction plan for quitting my job and starting the business. My extraction plan included strategically placed vacation days, education, and a few key milestones I knew I would have to meet before I was ready to board the "pink slip express" from my job. Folks who quickly left the district, or got fired, were known to have punched a ticket on the "pink slip express," which was a one-way trip to the unemployment line! My introduction to the market and preparation to start a business actually started prior to the birth of that extraction plan, back in 2002.

July 1, 2002, I took a job as the director of the design and construction department at a major school district in New Jersey. With close to 100 facilities—consisting of 86 schools and various technology centers, sports facilities and warehouses—an annual budget of over $990,000 was required to operate the organization. At the time, New Jersey's landmark Supreme Court decision, Abbott vs. Burke, declared that underserved school districts in New Jersey should receive the same funding for education and facilities as the "better off" suburban districts. Among other things, the Educational Facilities Construction and Finance Act of 1999 required the state of New Jersey to fund the Abbott school district's long-range facility plans (LRFP), including land acquisition, renovation costs and the construction of new school buildings and additions. In our district, the LRFP was valued at close to $1.6 billion, which involved building 40 new schools and 30 major renovations throughout the district, including approximately $100 million in local health and safety upgrade projects.

It was a great time to be in the center of all the action and I was there! But I knew that was not all that I wanted and still yearned for more. Before the end of the year, in August 2002 and after a consultation with my accountant, I had put my plan on paper and created my initial Limited Liability Company (LLC) filing to start my venture. Although I had no formal office, no dedicated phone line, and no employees—or customers for that matter—I had the beginning of my dream, in physical form.

In the school district I worked with a largely unionized workforce that included some very talented individuals who had been taxed by the system and were only concerned with doing enough to exist until retirement. It was really shocking to hear folks who had seemingly bright futures complain about their work environment and decide to do nothing but say, "I'll just keep quiet, do my next 14 years and retire." I can't say in all cases that I blame them for adopting that survival mentality in such a large organization. Working in large public agency environments requires you to play a numbers game of cost benefits analysis all the time. Considering the strong incentive of pensions, covered health care, and retirement savings, if you worked at one of the large agencies, it almost didn't make sense for you to leave after six or seven years. Many people, who probably had greater dreams, perhaps did the analysis and decided that, financially, it would be more worthwhile to stay there another 13 or 14 years, even if they were not happy with the conditions.

I knew I did not want to adopt that just-exist-until-retirement mentality so I had to have a plan to get out and get moving toward my own "stage" in a short period of time. I learned all I could about local politics and created all the relationships I had the opportunity to during those early years. I also filed and paid taxes on any consulting work that may have come my way during the initial years. Whatever I did was included in my new firm resume and recorded on my client job list since I knew I would be required to show actual clients I had worked for. Whether I was consulting with my church to find audio-visual professionals for a planned sanctuary sound system renovation

11

(new speakers) or providing advice and counsel on how to raise enough money to renovate the building's relief facilities (church bathrooms), it was included on my client job list. Even if someone asked for my opinion on local zoning ordinances and how they might approach their building plans, it was included on my client job list.

Believe it or not, a coworker at the time wanted to build a dog house in her back yard but was limited by rear yard and side setback zoning ordinances that restricted the size of the doghouse she could have built. I did say my business was construction management and perhaps you have heard the saying, "There is no job too big or too small." That was me in the beginning.

I reviewed her plans, consulted the zoning ordinance and instructed her on where to turn to petition the town for a zoning variance from the ordinance and how to select architectural professionals for her project. I know it was just a doghouse but this was the beginning of me providing my service to owners and clients who needed assistance and resources to pull together what was necessary to get their projects moving.

I continued to provide services for smaller, private projects and grossed about $2,500 in 2003, $7,500 in 2004, and about $11,000 in 2005. Not a whole lot of cash but certainly part of my extraction plan to show the track record necessary to obtain minority business certifications with state agencies. At that time the state division of commerce required you to have been in business at least three years and be able to prove you had filed tax returns showing activity or revenue for each of those years.

Next I calculated how I would market to my target audience after my initial business planning detailed my immediate needs. I knew I would need cash down the road and started to educate myself on buying investment property. My wife and I purchased our first investment property in 2002 for $75,000 in Hampton, Virginia and that purchase would become the genesis of start-up capital for my venture through a mortgage refinance. During that time I was on fire reading books and my favorite was *Rich Dad Poor Dad* by Robert Kiyosaki. I soaked up all I could on investment, money and business and received a pretty good financial education through my accountant/advisor and my self-study habits. While I was feeling good about how things were moving, I still didn't know when that magical time would come when I would be ready to quit my job and jump into entrepreneurship full time.

In December 2004 I received what I considered an unfair employee review from my boss and was very concerned about my future. I reached out to my support system, asked questions and, ultimately, requested a meeting with the superintendent of the school district to discuss what happened. Uncertain of how I would be received and unclear on what happened leading up to the meeting with the superintendent, I knew I would need to be prepared for the worst-case scenario—unplanned termination. As I prepared for the meeting, I envisioned it going down the way it happens in the movies—the young upstart professional walks into the boss' office, makes a couple of demands that fall on deaf ears, then whips out a prepared resignation letter and signs it on the spot! It looks like a pretty cool display of power when it happens in the movies.

My meeting did not go that way at all. However, I did walk in with a prepared resignation letter and thought I was prepared to pull it out and sign it if things didn't go my way. Well, I didn't use my letter on that day. Instead, during the conversation, which really wasn't a conversation at all, I quickly learned that the cards were not in my favor, considering the loyalty and relationships I thought I had built but, apparently, had not. The superintendent expressed his allegiance to my boss and told me I needed to work it out with him. I left his office dazed and amazed as I wrestled with how this would all work out. Not knowing when the right time would come to quit and launch the business, I continued to prepare and started to market more heavily for new opportunities. A couple of days later I was called into the business administrator's office. In a very casual manner I was told that the superintendent wanted my resignation because he felt I was no longer a team player. Wow! Ouch. I hadn't exactly expected it, but I had just been fired!

It was negotiated that I would stay on in my position until the end of the school year, June 30, 2005. I left the business administrator's office thankful that I had received my sign from God to move on to better things, but I felt very uneasy about the immediacy of it all. It was a shock because, while I had prepared for the possibility of being terminated and thought I was ready, what if I was not? Ready or not, though, it was indeed time for me to prepare to come to the stage with my bright ideas and concept for a new business. I summoned the courage to call my wife and tell her that I had just been liberated, but I knew she would be concerned as we had not had all the time we thought we needed to make sure we'd have a smooth transition. Nonetheless, my time in the district was up and it was time to perform on my own. While I tell folks I was ready to go and left the district to start my firm at just the right time, in reality I received a gigantic kick out the door from my boss.

Perhaps if I had not been pushed I might not have written this book. As my hysteria began to subside and the questions about how I would provide for my family faded, I heard that familiar call I knew required me to *make a bold move*, whether I was prepared or not: "Next, coming to the stage ... !

CHAPTER 1 - BOLD MOVES TO MAKE NOW!

* Be ready when the time comes by planning for it now!

* Don't worry about the recession, but focus on your breakthrough moment.

* Use your passion to propel you to the next level.

* Allow your good and bad circumstances to work for you.

* Negotiate a safe landing if and when you get pushed out of your comfort zone.

CHAPTER 2

DECIDING YOU WANT TO WIN BIG

With any venture you're considering starting or growing, you must first decide what you want out of it. In order for you to achieve your goals, you need to know what those goals are. In many cases you'll need to write them down and recite them each day and commit to achieving them. Are you working to enjoy a better lifestyle for you and your family or do you want to have a million dollars in the bank at the end of the first year? Are you preparing to live a millionaire lifestyle or are you going to live off the interest your million dollars generates?

I recently read *Crush It* by Gary Vaynerchuk, a businessman who has taken an established retail wine operation from $4 million a year in sales to over $64 million in sales in less than four years. And he says he wants to buy the New York Jets football franchise. His determination to be successful is the reason he is in business and at least one of his main goals involves buying the New York Jets. Take a look at Facebook co-founder Mark Zuckerberg whose wildly successful Internet utility is now worth an estimated $50 billion, according to CNBC. Zuckerberg often says, "It's not about the money or getting rich, I just want to change the world." They both have goals in mind and both are seemingly well on their way to achieving them, all while enjoying the benefits of successful business operations.

So what is your version of success? Will you be driving fancy cars and wearing designer clothes or will you live like the "millionaire next door," shopping at discount retailers like Wal-Mart and Target? I prefer the discount retailers over the department stores on most days, but I'll admit—perhaps like some of you—that I, too, want the shine and bling that comes with being successful.

I will tell you that I have wanted to buy the Mercedes-Benz S550 for three years now but can't bring myself to make the purchase. I have studied the car, been to the dealership to drive it and searched options and available inventory models from New Jersey all the way to California. I would not mind flying to California to purchase my car then driving it back—or better yet, shipping it to my home in New Jersey. But I am not yet prepared to do that. I can buy the car, valued at $110,000, but my money management and better sense say, *There are still other things that I want out of this business venture that take priority at this time over a very nice, but hugely depreciable, asset.*

Believe me, there will be a time when you see me driving that car or some other high-end car, but it will be slightly used and paid for in cash or purchased as a tax strategy and nothing else. Smart money moves, and a bit of delayed gratification is what will sustain you and your venture and accommodate your version of success.

Starting your venture will require you to gauge your definition of success. Is it about fame, fortune, notoriety, or none of the above? Is your picture of success having the financial freedom to do all the things in life you want to do and when you want to do them? Is your picture of success having all the things you have not yet had but still want? Or does it involve philanthropic initiatives where you would give away most of what you build, living only off of the 10% to 20% that you might really need to survive?

My definition of success is having a great balance of health, family, business, and personal pursuits on my terms, which means, among other things, that if I want to take my family to Hawaii for Thanksgiving, we are going! If I want to take a three-week vacation from my daily routine and play golf every day, then it will happen. If I want to pay all of my bills electronically on an automatic calendar schedule for the year, then let it happen. For some folks, just being able to pay their bills on time without worry is their definition of success. Of course, everyone wants the bills paid without having to worry about them, but imagine if you could actually decide on it and make it happen? Our bills are getting paid but I wouldn't exactly say I don't worry about them—which I think is normal since I believe that a little focused paranoia and concern is always good for motivation.

Being clear about your version of success is critical because if you don't have it figured out relatively early in your journey, you may miss what success really is for you. Instantly, your firm makes $5 million after three years in business but now you work 120 hours a week and have no time for your family—what a tragedy! You win a five-year performance contract based on your personal involvement and suddenly you are stricken with a health concern that puts you on bed rest for a year—what a tragedy! You are the darling of the press and appear on several media outlets to tell your success story but are going through a painful divorce and family breakup that consumes you every hour of the day—what a tragedy! Unfortunately, these scenarios occur quite frequently with business owners, and just because you don't plan on them happening doesn't mean they won't.

Deciding on winning and what your personal pursuit and image of success truly is will hopefully keep you focused on what matters most on your journey and keep you from losing sight of what you are really doing this for. In addition to wanting a multimillion-dollar construction management firm, I also decided that I needed to preserve my family life and my wonderful marriage, and not miss my children growing up. When you do decide what you want out of your business, please don't forget to share your vision with your spouse and obtain their buy-in and support. For all my actions and efforts, time and money would not be available for the business if it were not for the tremendous sacrifice and love of my beautiful wife, Jennifer, who is also an entrepreneur of over 10 years. I have her support and she has mine, and we truly understand how to work together and praise each other's ventures and businesses, which do take up a lot of our time and energy. We enjoy the fruits of our businesses and our marriage of over 17 years, and will soon begin regularly sharing our lessons learned on our BlogTalk Radio show, Business Bliss-Marital Success at www.blogtalkradio.com/businessblissmaritalsuccess.

Having worked for several large construction management firms in the New York City market by the time I started my own CM firm, I knew I wanted to hit it big. After all, we are taught to have it all or, at least, to want it all in business. I decided I wanted to build a $100 million company within 10 years. A tremendous goal, I admit, but I have never been shy about my business pursuits or tried to deny my aggressive nature when it comes to attempting to reach the goals I set. I was told that if you want to be "big business," you have to start looking, acting, and thinking like "big business." I started my quest to look, act, and think like a "big business" even before I had earned a dime. I spent a lot of time studying successful businesses and, to this day, still read business biographies every opportunity I get.

Armed with a great concept for a new construction management firm, in depth knowledge of how the industry worked, a professional work ethic and credible reputation, and a minority business certification (which is critical for public contracts), I began the process of marketing to mega-construction firms in late 2004. At the time I still had a full-time job, but I knew enough to start my firm on paper two years earlier. When seeking business certifications, you may be required to have been in business for at least two to three years before you can be considered.

When I started my last full-time job in 2002 where I was making $118,000 per year, I knew I wanted to quit after approximately three or four years. I joined the school district as director of the Design and Construction Department, responsible for the planning, management and implementation of the long-range facility plan, which consisted of building 40 new schools and completing 30 major renovations/additions valued at approximately $1.6 billion. I mentioned earlier that I was never shy about my pursuits and stepping up to challenges, so I felt right at home in the flurry of activity that came with this assignment. The math was easy: Since I began the assignment in 2002, I had to quit in 2005 to build my business and grow to $100 million by 2015.

So there I was, preparing to make a "bold move" after securing my first MBE certification in late 2004. I positioned our newly created firm in the crux of the New Jersey construction market while I was still employed. The state of New Jersey was planning a new forensic science lab for the State Trooper Police Force. It was a $100 million project and I thought, *Wow! This was my plan exactly.* But how would I get started or even get close to winning this project just having started the firm a few months prior. While I was hopeful, I pretty much figured we would not get a chance to work on this project. But I did see value in attending the mandatory pre-proposal conference to learn about the details of the project and submission requirements. This decision was beneficial on two major levels. First, it allowed me to see the requirements for submission on a $100 million project, and second and most important, I knew that anyone who was a player in the industry and looking for work would be at this pre-proposal conference.

It became a huge marketing opportunity, being able to let every one of my contacts and some new contacts know that I was leaving the school district, had started my own firm, and was ready to partner with them for work. It turned out to be a brilliant plan. I planned to use my vacation days to attend the pre-proposal conferences to market myself. I quickly encouraged and deputized my close friend and college fraternity brother of almost 20 years, Ceylon Frett, to assist me in attending these events to present us as a true team with resources. Even though he was a full-time employee of another firm at the time, Ceylon Frett was also my director of business development. He had worked in promotions and marketing for various entertainments companies, including Mercury Records, and really knew the art of dealing with people, as well as influencing product development and sales. I had often talked to Ceylon about my passion to develop this new company and here was our first chance.

> **MAKE A BOLD MOVE**
>
> *Use pre-proposal conferences as marketing opportunities, even if you can't win the project. Take a calculated risk and enter a market you probably don't deserve to be in—if looking only at experience or business stature. Use the opportunity to market your firm to the folks who have a real chance to win, or who can't win but are still major players.*

Remember, even though we had only existed on paper and I hadn't quit my job at the district yet, I was the President & CEO and had a marketing professional attending meetings with me. Needless to say, we didn't win the $100 million forensic science lab project. But of the approximately 90 high-level professionals representing CM firms in attendance, I did connect with an industry veteran I'd known for many years. He was a vice president for a major mega-CM firm and I got a chance to make an appointment with him to discuss our start-up.

The VP's name is Phil Rollins and I had known him for quite some time; I had supervised his contract and scope of work when he worked at my former agency in the late 90s. Then, Phil was working for a large construction company that also had ties to my former agency. Now, Phil was working for a leading construction and engineering firm in New York. He invited me to his office to discuss my transition and new venture. Armed with marketing brochures and the gift of gab, I took the meeting to get up to speed about how large firms work and to find out what their needs might be in order to find my niche. After talking for about 30 minutes about various project opportunities and having the edge of knowing about new projects before anyone else, Phil hit me with a proposition. He mentioned that his firm had relationships in place and were dealing with a few quality minority businesses already, but if we had knowledge of something new coming out and the situation was right, they might discuss pursuing opportunities with us as their sub-consultant. The meeting ended with Phil saying, "Well, if you find something out there that we can work on together, bring it to us and let's discuss it."

At the time, I thought, *this is crap*! I am leaving my job to start my own business and all I end up with is a noncommissioned external sales position with one of the largest firms in the country. It felt like I had given up a secure position and future to go out and search for opportunities to bring to a megafirm—for free. But what I was actually doing was building my niche and making myself more valuable to larger firms than my own.

Since I had decided to win big and knew I had to grow my firm quickly, I took Phil's challenge to find something out there that we could work on together. It felt like unpaid, disconnected sales prospecting for them—not me. Then I came to realize that if, in fact, I could create a situation where they needed me as much as or more than I needed them, perhaps this arrangement could work. After doing research on Phil's firm and what clients they had, I learned that while they had a great deal of success on huge construction projects in New York City, there were a few projects that they wanted badly but had not won, to date. I discovered that my past relationships at the agency I used to work for would be the key to creating a need for this megafirm to work with my start-up.

I got in touch with my contacts who still worked at my old firm and dug for information. A lot of the folks I had worked with from 1990 to 2001 were still there and, in a lot of cases, had been promoted. I used my knowledge of their system for access and quickly learned the "behind-the-scenes" info about firms that were "hot" and winning large contracts at the agency and what was necessary for them to win. Since the agency was serious about minority business, it quickly became apparent that if a mega-firm was going to win a contract, they needed a willing, recognizable minority business enterprise (MBE) on their team.

Here was my chance to build toward my goal of $100 million and win big from the start. A new contract for the agency—which was to promote opportunities for growth to minority-owned, women-owned and locally based businesses in New York City—was coming up for renewal and there was a solid chance for at least two new firms to win contracts.

By now I had also enlisted the support of another friend and mentor of over 10 years who I had worked with over the years, Johnnie B. Harris, Jr. I had worked for Johnnie when he was a project officer at my former agency in the early 1990s. He had a wealth of knowledge and was a trusted resource, which led me to recruit him to work for me in the Office of Design and Construction at the school district in 2003, after he'd left the agency. Johnnie also had in-depth knowledge of how the agency worked and I thought it would be critical to have his efforts on our team and increase our credibility. I never was able to utilize Johnnie in as great a capacity as he'd been used at the agency but I felt it valuable to have him on the team. His insight and wisdom always resonated with me and I appreciated his reasoning.

> **MAKE A BOLD MOVE**
>
> *Don't be afraid to negotiate a huge winning position with a major firm just because you are starting from the bottom. Find your competitive advantage, your unique selling position, or identify critical relationships that can create a win on any level, and exploit them for a major portion of a contract when teaming with a major force in the industry.*

The contract we pursued was for $30 million over a two-year period with a renewable third year option. We brought the opportunity and a real business strategy back to Phil's firm and negotiated a 30% position on the contract if we won the deal. This was unheard of since most MBE contracts had around 15% to 20% involvement. Since I knew the agency specifics and could be instrumental in winning the deal, we negotiated up from Phil's firm's starting offer of 15%, along with a bunch of other specific incentives and guidelines that we knew we could count on to grow our firm to our present success. In early 2006 we were awarded a $30 million contract of which we had 30% of the deal. This was the contract that allowed us to win big from the start and we are still working on this contract almost six years later. We took a chance and partnered with Phil's firm and our relationship has grown and they have supported our success on various projects.

Phil's firm is international with over 46,000 employees working in over 40 countries. The firm's 2009 revenues were approximately $9.25 billion. The company provides program management; planning, design, and engineering; systems engineering and technical assistance; construction and construction management; operations and maintenance; and decommissioning and closure services. Together, my firm and Phil's firm have formed a great work strategy, completed approximately $200 million in projects for the agency and been largely responsible for developing and implementing successful projects in their new programs throughout New York City. Together, we have created metrics for other firms to be measured by and have "written the book on emerging contractor development."

In October 2010 we won a new training contract with the agency where we are the prime contractor and Phil's firm is our sub-consultant. Not bad for a 25-person emerging firm that didn't even exist 10 years ago. We are effectively turning the tables on the industry, delivering value and results for clients and creating wins for us all. Remember, the 46,000-employee behemoth that we are working side-by-side with is also surviving and thriving off of our solutions, and we all benefit greatly from the joint work we do together.

It all started with thinking big from the beginning and making the decision to look, act, and think like the firm we would become. With an aggressive goal in mind and on paper, we shot for the stars and are still climbing, well on our way to our planned success.

While we are not yet a $100 million company, we successfully contributed to winning a $100 million contract in 2007 and went on to successfully renew that contract in 2008, which was valued at an additional $60 million. By the time you read this, we hope to have secured our third renewal on this project but, this time, not as a major sub-consultant but as a full joint-venture partner on a proposed contract valued at $75 million.

We, of course, plan on winning this mega-deal but, as a 50/50 joint-venture partner, we will not only be counting our portion of the contract staffing dollars but also the indirect costs, consumables, and most of all, the profit. Furthermore, as a joint-venture partner, half of this entire contract will be regarded as our revenue, which immediately gives us an edge on quickly becoming an $18 million to $20 million firm sometime before the end of 2012, based solely on the revenue from this single contract. Now how's that for thinking big and deciding up front that you want to win right now? Make your decision to win big, think big, and be "big business", if that's your version of success. It was my decision to win big and think big, and it still is!

CHAPTER 2 - BOLD MOVES TO MAKE NOW!

* Think big from the start!

* Confirm what your version of success really is.

* Decide now what you want most out of your venture.

* Research the firms that are where you want to be.

* Put yourself in the room with the people and firms that can get you to the next level.

* Visualize your firm performing on that level and speak it into existence!

CHAPTER 3

PLANNING TO BE SUCCESSFUL

Failing to plan is surely planning to fail. Believe it or not, this rings true on most accounts in many businesses. A few lucky folks fall into business success either through timing, inheritance or by chance, if you believe your path can be determined by any of those. But most of us have to have solid plans. According to 2004 U.S. Census Bureau statistics, there were approximately 25 million small businesses in the U.S. but over 77% of them were listed as non-employer firms, operating unincorporated, or operating without any payroll. I would suggest that this overwhelming majority of firms are in business with no plan for directional growth or success. Furthermore, of the remaining 5.8 million U.S. businesses, or 23% of the total (about 47% of that category—2.7 million) operated with between one and four employees, which was the largest sector of small businesses in the U.S. economy in 2004. This is your competition. If they are planning and you are not, it will not take long for your bright ideas to be tested. However, if you can get the planning process right, your chances are greatly improved for sustainability and success.

Business Success Planning

The business planning process can be mechanical and arduous, and perhaps that's why most people would rather not begin it. However, one of the most crucial lessons our firm learned over the course of our initial five years was that building solid plans and planning to be successful are two different things. Ultimately, we all hope the plan we build yields success, but we cannot forget to plan for that success and be prepared once it arrives. You can get to the top with sheer muscle and good fortune but that usually won't keep you there. Solid and strategic business planning is what will work and keep you on pace to reach your goals, no matter what they are.

A solid business plan will consist of several specific items, goals, and directions, but it should also be a living document, constantly updated and refreshed. You should be able to refer back to your business goals when contemplating decisions for new clients or marketing decisions. You should also be able to consult your business plan to develop a recruitment effort consistent with where your firm will operate and what your core competency will ultimately be. In addition to the standard items in your business plan, be sure to cover the following in detail:

* **Market Identification & Segmentation:** Where your product, service, or experience will exist in the marketplace and which market you will reach.

* **Market Analysis:** Supply and demand and discussion of alternatives for your product, service, or experience and how you will fill a void or need in the identified marketplace.

* **Identification of Your Product, Service or Experience:** A detailed description of what you are selling, why it's important, and what value it can create for the target market.

* **Unique Selling Position:** Your differentiation and/or competitive advantage over the existing competition and how you will successfully exist amidst that competition.

* **Industry Background:** Frame the market for folks outside of your industry. Identify industry leaders, recent changes, pending legislation, and current competition.

* **Management Team & Resources:** A description of the professionals you have identified to build and sustain your management team, understanding that no one will believe you can do it all on your own.

* **Location & Region of Operations:** The challenges and potential rewards of operating in a particular region or specific locale. Explain the value in knowing the customs, clients, and conditions of local markets.

* **Target Market Consumer/Client Designation:** Who your product, service, or experience is designed for, including affinity, demographic or the entity that needs it most, and the potential fringe or secondary target that can also benefit.

* **Sales & Marketing Strategy:** How to best position your message to your target market to build market share, as well as your positioning in the industry for recognition and business opportunities to sell.

✳ **Technology Focus:** How you will harness technology to ramp up or operate your strategy, and the cost, rewards, benefits and pitfalls of its use across your organization.

✳ **Financing & Business Capital:** Indicate the initial and long-term capital needs of the venture as well as detailed costs, expenditures, sources, and uses of funds. Also describe the staging of financing required to support the venture.

✳ **Growth Projections & Revenue:** Projected sales and revenue data year-to-year and customer retention rates based on lead-generating activities, business development and industry customs.

The planning process not only allows you to identify everything your potential investors need to know about your business but it also causes you to contemplate some of your early assumptions. The market conditions in your industry—a recession or intense competition from rivals, for example—can cause you to question the validity of your plan and may require you to adjust it. This plan becomes a roadmap that can be used as a reminder of who you are, where you're going and, ultimately, where you want to be.

> **MAKE A BOLD MOVE**
>
> *Plan for your success on family, personal, and business levels to achieve buy-in from the people who matter most and from those who will ultimately support your efforts to achieve your goals. Become an ambassador of the life you expect to have while living your dreams and others will be attracted to that, providing much needed support and encouragement.*

Family Success Planning

While you will be supported by any of the current business planning software applications that can guide you through this planning process, you will still need to *coordinate your family, personal, and business life for the success you desire.* Planning to be successful with your family doesn't mean constantly stating, "In order for us to live in this house or drive this car, I have to keep working and won't be around for family functions!" Do not ask your family to count you out. But do count them in and ask them to be a part of your coming success.

Planning for your success with your family might include inviting them to attend business conferences where they can all connect with people sharing similar attitudes toward life and money. This might sound expensive considering that business conferences usually have a registration fee, not to mention the cost of hotel accommodations and travel arrangements. Further burning up your cash will be meals, entertainment and, in some cases, childcare if you have younger children that will need to be looked after while you are networking. Even though this may require additional money, do not miss the value of bringing your family to the table, not only to keep them close to your success but also to teach important lessons on entrepreneurship, financial literacy, and generational wealth accumulation.

In building NobleStrategy, I have decided to plan for success early. I have long wanted to be on the cover of *Black Enterprise* magazine and continue to work toward that goal. Growing up reading the magazine, I always enjoyed the business success showcased on those pages. It gave me aspirations of one day succeeding on that level. Of course, in order to be featured in *Black Enterprise* one day, you would have to start reading *Black Enterprise* now! I began reading the magazine at the early age of about 16. As I learned from the lessons in the magazine and became familiar with the stories, I envisioned one day having my face on the cover and my company featured. It may have seemed far-fetched but I planned for success, started to consume the information in the magazine, and attended my first Entrepreneurs Conference in Dallas, Texas in 2004.

I urged my wife, who is also a business owner of over 10 years, as well as an accomplished scientist, having earned her Ph.D. in pathology in 1999, to attend. Prior to attending the conference, I'd always said I wanted to go but was too concerned with the cost. Registration was nearly $600 and did not include hotel accommodations, travel, or meals. I knew it would be costly for my wife and me to attend; however, I made the sacrifice. That first Black Enterprise Entrepreneurs Conference was groundbreaking for me and pushed me to the point of preparing my business so I could quit my job! Not only did I get some great information at the conference but the effect of networking with folks who had similar vision and folks who had already been successful was immeasurable. We soaked up the information and read the recommended books; we attended the seminars and established the relationships that would propel both of our businesses to where we are now.

Unknowingly, the relationships we forged at our first Black Enterprise Conference in 2004 would be critical to the growth NobleStrategy experienced in 2009. You can never be certain about how and when key meetings will create personal and professional opportunities.

My bold move was not worrying about the cost of the event and the expenses I would incur, even though my business had not started yet. Instead, I focused on the value of investing in being where I needed to be to align myself with the professionals that were doing what I so badly wanted to do. I jumped in and quickly obtained the education, skills, relationships, and fuel I needed to get the business started, with my wife in attendance as well, in order to properly plan to share my success.

Although it may initially cost you to plan for success, the return on your investment will be immeasurable and help you reach your goals.

Even today, almost eight years after that initial "family conference," I utilize this concept to encourage my children to not only understand what I do but also develop similar attitudes about money and financial freedom. Recently, our family returned from a Black Enterprise Golf and Tennis challenge, which was held at a luxurious resort and spa. We spent the Labor Day weekend playing golf, going to the spa, networking and enjoying nightly entertainment with folks just as serious as we are about living our dreams. The registration cost for the event was $900 per person, but access to the network of people that attended and the opportunity to make new contacts made the fee well worth it.

It does make a difference if you equip children at a young age to expect certain things out of life in return for their hard and smart work. We value working hard and playing hard, so while the conference is business-related, it also served as another lesson for my family in planning for success. As long as my children can learn the value of business concepts, associations, networking, and relationships at an early age, I am confident they, too, will be successful and lead the lives they desire on their own terms.

Personal Success Planning

Planning for success in your personal life is equally important. If you want to lead an organization that implements a winning plan and a long-term growth strategy over the next 10 years, you must make sure you're here for the next 10 years. You will need to manage your health and spirit to ensure that you effectively execute your plan for success. Even when you do all you can, there are no guarantees. But you will feel better about improving your odds and chances for longevity. In my case, managing my health and spirit means attending 6:00 a.m. fitness boot camp three to four days a week during the spring and summer months.

I used to be consumed with the day-to-day activities of running the business and often started very early and worked very late to accomplish all that was required each day. I have come to learn that no matter what time you start, there is always more to do when you operate your own business. So you need to work aggressively but with a plan of action that can be sustained. Now I rise at 5:30 a.m. to work out at boot camp before work, which makes me very tired but strengthens and conditions my body for the hard work and stress that comes with the level of success I desire. I am not down to a svelte 225 pounds yet—actually not even down to 300 pounds yet. But remember, muscle *is* heavier than fat! I'm on my way and consciously planning for my success right now ...

Once we arrive at our $100 million in revenue (which is projected for 2015), perhaps then it will be time for me to relinquish my role as president & CEO and create new goals and directions. To that end I am planning for success in my business life by equipping my firm with structure and processes that will allow continuation and sustainability.

Do you know that less than 30% of all Americans have wills? We've already learned that 77% of U.S. businesses operate with no payroll and very likely no plan. So what percentage of them do you think have made plans for succession or continuation? One of the concepts that I am exploring use of in the coming years in order to sustain our business is the Employee Stock Ownership Plan (ESOP). While they are very intricate, ESOPs provide great business benefits, such as allowing the ESOP entity to borrow funds that can be used for the business while deducting principle and interest payments during loan payback for tax purposes. An ESOP can also provide the necessary funds to finance an expansion and provide for capital needs or the acquisition of other firms, which are all on the table for NobleStrategy.

The 113-year-old industry powerhouse Tishman Construction was acquired for $245 million by AECOM Technology Corporation. It was a cash and stock deal, largely supported by the use of AECOM's 2007 initial public offering, which was aided by their ESOP, fueling their growth of over 473% since 1990 and revenues of approximately $6.5 billion in 2010. Those are the kinds of numbers that we currently dream of. But in order to achieve that success, we must plan for it. Studying other firms who have been successful and learning from their template is what we believe in and it's what we recommend. With a well thought out plan—a plan built for success, with an eye on what is actually taking place in your industry and what matters most to you—it can happen. I am determined to achieve major goals while maintaining my family, personal, and business ideals of success.

Think about your strategy for where you want your business success to take you and your family and how your goals will be achieved. Then commit to making it happen.

My experiences have provided a great deal of satisfaction and reward in my life, but one of the things I enjoy the most is teaching entrepreneurship to children. Part of the reason is their simplistic attitudes toward things we adults make very complex. In teaching children how to plan for success, I ask them to create vision boards of what they want in the future. It always helps to have a vision for where you want to go and to take every opportunity to learn from others' mistakes and use their success to fuel your drive. I am confident that we will put deals together to acquire other firms in our quest for growth, but AECOM's purchase of a 113-year-old legacy firm creates countless opportunities for learning and business emulation.

It brings to mind that familiar adage: If you can see it, you can achieve it. I have revised that saying and ask that you repeat it as your mantra: *See it, say it, believe it, and achieve it.*

We will come back to that in a few chapters but the meaning is consistent. In order to get where you're going, you must know or, at least, have some idea of what that place looks like. Once you visualize your ideas you can plan for your success by *making bold moves* as outlined here to gain your financial freedom and live your dreams.

CHAPTER 3 - BOLD MOVES TO MAKE NOW!

* Immediately build a plan for success.

* Create a vision board of what that success looks like.

* Have clear targets and goals as part of your plan.

* Prepare yourself and your family for the rigors of success.

* Use your business to teach financial literacy and other lessons to your children.

* Study successful firms and learn from the techniques they employ.

* Invest today in relationships you plan on leveraging tomorrow.

* Map out the technical aspects of your proposition, market, business model and required financing.

* Maintain your personal health in preparation for your increased personal wealth.

* Decide now what you want most out of your venture.

CHAPTER 4

GETTING PAID NOW AND MORE LATER

If you have recently started your business, you have probably heard friends and family counsel you not to quit your day job until you get enough money coming in to pay the bills. Unfortunately, I haven't seen it work in this manner at all. As long as you are tied to your day job, you will likely never have the passion, hunger, momentum, or desperation to make something happen for your own venture, on your own terms. Furthermore, if serving two masters does work for you temporarily, you will quickly brand yourself as someone who is not very serious about his business and is not even willing to invest in himself. Not many clients will accept propositions to make an investment in or with anyone who is not invested in themselves.

So how do you quit your day job and generate enough cash to grow your business and keep the lights on today and tomorrow? It's a very tricky situation, but folks like you navigate it every day.

Read on to find a few strategies for combating slow money and to assist you in the planning process so you can get paid now—and even more later.

> **MAKE A BOLD MOVE**
>
> *Instead of trying to build your vision while working a full-time job, commit to quit your day job and build a plan to market your excess time while your business clients are developing. Create a related performance business that ties into a fringe market that you can support based on your own skills, expertise, and excess time.*

Develop a Related Performance Business

Being encouraged to think big will produce huge ideas and concepts to be fulfilled in your company venture. But while building up to your vision, find an opportunity that may be related to your main business that you can perform on your own time, without relying on anyone else.

One of the things you will surely have once you make the commitment to quit your day job is free time. You will need a plan to use this free time effectively. I can remember when I quit my day job in the spring of 2005; I experienced a euphoria that I can not explain. It has to do with conquering your fears and stepping into a space that is very uncomfortable, unpredictable and that will cause you to rely on your resourcefulness. It's definitely a *bold move* and it feels real good when you first do it. I was on top of the world and it felt like I literally floated for about two weeks.

During this time I got to promote my newfound independence and catch up on all the things that working a 9-to-5 seems to make impossible. And even though my activity was nonstop in developing my new company—designing brochures, purchasing computers, researching projects and clients, recruiting potential talent and finding my unique selling position—there was always excess time. I planned to meet with at least four potential clients each day, two in the morning and two in the evening, which is a frantic pace. Imagine driving to your 9:00 a.m. meeting then conducting the presentation at your 11:00 a.m. appointment, grabbing a quick bite to eat, then dashing off to your 1:00 p.m. and your 3:00 p.m. before wrapping up. And the day still allows time to respond to clients' questions and produce proposals, presentations and set appointments for the rest of the week. After you stick to this schedule for three or four days, you will feel like you need a break. Furthermore, after all the cold-calling, marketing, advertising, and promoting, you will have to wait on calls to come in—and the phone is not yet ringing.

Despair can creep in. To ward it off you begin looking for diversions. I can remember having so much down time that I actually went to the local cinema and tried to watch three movies in one day. I couldn't do it. Have you ever had so much free time that you would contemplate going to an 11:00 a.m. movie, then watching another at 2:00 p.m. then another at 4:45 p.m., all in one day? A painful use of your free time, but as you build you will have very slow periods and will need to manage your impulse to keep moving.

Marketing to large public agency clients during the day, I needed to make use of my excess time while I waited for that huge contract opportunity. I decided to pursue a fringe market to the commercial construction management market—the residential real estate inspection services area. Having been in the midst of a soon-to-decline housing boom in late 2005, I knew that the market was filled with investment activity, such as home sales and purchases. Since I was selling construction management and inspection services to my larger commercial clients, I was able to see the void in the residential real estate market that could be adapted for a major opportunity. I had the benefit of being a construction professional with over 20 years experience in the market, which I knew was a credible selling point. And I had worked for some of the largest construction agencies in the New York City metropolitan area, which I also knew would be marketable. I quickly developed a reporting and presentation format for project inspections that was similar to reporting used on large agency construction programs. Even though I had an undergraduate degree in Building Construction Technology, a graduate degree in Management of Technology and 20 years of market experience, I still did not have the formal credentials to perform home inspections. I saw the market opportunity and welcomed the chance to adapt to the fringe market of residential home inspections.

After further investigation, I learned that inspections in my state could only be performed by certified home inspectors, professional engineers or registered architects. In order to be certified as a home inspector, I would have to take a lengthy course and work approximately 1,000 hours under the tutelage of another certified home inspector. I had no time for that and concluded that it just wouldn't work. Instead, my plan was to engage a local registered architect to review the field inspection form that I had put together and have the registered architect (RA) sign off on the final prepared document. It worked like a charm. I was able to charge slightly more than a home inspector for this enhanced construction consulting report signed by a registered architect and compiled by a 20-year construction industry veteran.

I marketed my services to real estate attorneys who were often asked by buyers where they could get a reputable firm to perform their inspections. I wound up satisfying a number of clients and became the main referral for construction consulting reporting for a major real estate attorney in northern New Jersey. While this was not glamorous work, it allowed me to make great use of my excess time, use my skills and earn enough money to keep the lights on until the high-paying job opportunities found their way to my desk. I wasn't so thrilled to be crawling around a dark, musty basement that would be some newly married couple's first home, but it allowed me to market and sustain myself without the cost of paying for performance services.

This concept worked for me and can work for you, to tide you over until the real money comes in. Even though you have big dreams, you still need to get paid now. You can worry about getting paid more later.

Utilize a Concept from an Alternate Industry: Factoring

Cash flow is crucial to growing any business. Businesses need this financial lifeline to run operations smoothly. One wrong move in cash flow could spell instant disaster for any firm—from the largest to the smallest. But when first starting out, it won't always be as simple as making sure you get paid for your services.

Entrepreneurs spend a great deal of time working to win the contract, but we must have the same focus in getting paid.

In teaching children the fundamentals of entrepreneurship, we play a game called Pay Me Now! Basically, it's BINGO with financial concepts. Children have to understand the definitions of certain business terms and then be able to spot when they have successfully crossed off a successive row as the terms are called out. The game's lesson is two-fold. In addition to recognizing and understanding the terms, the critical object of the game is to recognize when you must get paid. Just like in BINGO, if you don't call it, you don't get it.

I train children as young as age four to know when they are supposed to get paid, and I encourage them to emphatically yell out "Pay me now!" when that moment comes. Similarly, when operating a business, if your thought is, *I'll just do a good job and the client will recognize my efforts and pay me in a timely manner*, you will be in for a major surprise and some negative cash flow problems. Our teaching lesson confirms that no one is willing to pay you when you don't even know when you are supposed to be paid. Also, oftentimes, if you don't make it your business to ask, clients will go about their regular routine and pay you in their normal course of business, whenever they get to it. If that works for you, then you don't need to read anymore of this. Just go on your merry way and enjoy the rest of your short business life. However, if getting paid is your focus and you are in tune with it, examine the next step for continued growth on a major level.

How can effectively selling large clients affect your business? One of the quickest paths to growth and market penetration is to land a "big fish" client. But working with that "big fish" client takes a new skill set in performing adequately and getting paid, and ensuring that the breadth of the contract doesn't consume your cash flow and available resources. If you are selling to a reputable agency that can be vetted by business industry analysts, such as Dun & Bradstreet®, you can probably utilize a factoring approach or accounts receivable financing to get paid.

Large construction agencies will often pay contractors in 60, 90, or 120-day terms, depending on their approval and payment process. With the opportunity for growth and the need to pay several employees for what could amount to three months of payroll, taxes, salary and benefits, selling invoices or utilizing a factor for advance payment becomes very necessary. Factoring or receivable financing is used by businesses to convert sales on credit terms for immediate cash flow. Financing accounts receivable is a very flexible method of achieving required working capital for businesses of all sizes. Basically, a business sells an invoice or a portion of their accounts receivable to a funding party—factoring agent—at a discount, in order to receive a percentage of the cash for the invoice immediately. The good news is that the determination to accept the invoice is based on the strength of the buyer and not the seller, who is strapped for cash. Furthermore, factoring involves three parties in the deal as opposed to a traditional bank loan which involves only two.

During our firm's first three years, we operated without traditional bank financing. We were not able to secure a bank loan or a line of credit initially because we did not fit into the financial industry's formula for financing businesses. Our business was not yet five years old and we did not have the traditional mix of clients in different sectors that banks look for. Instead of having one large client, banks like to see you with a traditional mix of clients and sectors in an effort to shelter themselves from one big deal going bad. If it were up to the

37

banks, I would have derived about 20% of my revenue from large private clients, about 20% from smaller private clients, another 20% from public clients, perhaps another 20% from nonprofits, and maybe another 20% from federal contracts. This way, if there is a downturn in the economy where a particular sector gets hit hard, the bank can recover based on the revenue from other sources.

Banks will only fund seemingly perfect scenarios where, on paper, the risk is virtually nonexistent. We landed a big fish and that agency represented roughly 75% of our firm's revenue. This frightened traditional banks but made us very glad. First the banks told me, *"You are not yet established and you need more work history before we can finance you."* Then they told me, *"Well, you have been around long enough but haven't made significant revenue to support your venture."* Then they said, *"You have been around long enough and have the sales to support a loan, but you actually grew too fast."* I could not believe my ears! We grew too fast! For most entrepreneurs who quit their day jobs, growing too fast in 24 months or less is not typically on the list of things to be concerned about. This is one of those problems entrepreneurs would probably pay to have when trying to get started. Here the banks were, rejecting me because *"we grew too fast"*.

To this day, my perception of most bankers is not very good. And I really disagree with most of their thinking, especially the traditional banks. In this market, banks really don't show much incentive to create opportunities for you to grow your firm because they can continue making fees off of consumer banking products. In this scenario, they never need to invest in community or commercially viable loans for local business, which seems to conflict with their position in the local market and all the community lending advertising some banks do. Community banks make much more sense and are often willing to invest in the business concept and the individual, to make a calculated risk in growing their money with you. You should not be discouraged, though, because you can still fund your business on a large scale. It will just cost you a little bit more than a traditional loan or line of credit.

When we won our first $30 million contract, less than 12 months from when I quit my full-time job, we needed to send several people to work and wait several months for our money.

After securing a $10,000 loan from a community business lender —which only covered the very first payroll—we turned to a factoring company that provided us with 70% of an invoice within four days, after we submitted a verifiable invoice to the client. They took a hefty share of the deal, and each invoice was treated separately. But this process at least allowed us to enter a huge market and become a player, without ever really having the financial resources traditionally utilized to do it.

Those initial deals cost us about 3% for the 30-day period until the client paid, and then 1% every 10 days after that the invoice was outstanding. If you were to get paid after 120 days, you would be charged a whopping 12% against an invoice for one bi-weekly period where your services were provided to a client. On an approved invoice of $36,000, the fees to factor that invoice would run approximately $4,320, and that does not include wire fees, express mail, etc.

The process was very mechanical and required a series of faxes, approvals and client sign-offs before you could get funded. With all of its issues and expenses, I am very thankful that we were able to use the factor when we started. It was an easy decision to give up more money for the resources—in this case, cash to advance a client's contract—rather than not fulfill the contract at all because our cash flow wouldn't support it.

We no longer need to use factoring and have secured traditional financing, but thanks to an understanding of the appropriate products, I had the opportunity to make a business decision that supported our growth in a major way.

Establish a Financial Profile/Credit History with Business Industry Analysts

One of the quickest ways to establish your firm is to register with a financial or business industry analytical service such as Dun & Bradstreet®. These services are vital in establishing business credit and a financial snapshot for clients interested in validating you and your service, or determining what threshold of credit or financial risk you might actually be. They can also be very helpful to entrepreneurs in migrating their personal credit history over to a business credit profile, which is usually necessary since personal credit is the only credit history most people can show starting out.

For most start-ups, the business is essentially tied to an individual. But there must be a plan to move your business toward independence from you. While you will be required to sign personal guarantees and become a personal debtor on many business loans, you should always be working to move to a permanent corporate model that will support itself. It will take time to establish the profile required to gain full independence as a new entity, but this must be the plan from which you operate. You will be required to pledge personal collateral for some business financing—such as your home, receivables, or cash instruments—until you reach the point of comfort with the traditionally established banking community.

Earlier we discussed the need to be able to invest in yourself and take a calculated risk, showing your clients and potential investors that you are fully committed. And it doesn't get more committed than pledging your house or investment properties, or even your stream of cash receivables to the bank in order to secure your deal. No one likes this, but how do you move forward without doing it?! Use these tools, no matter how demanding, as motivation to make your company an independent entity, and work each day to get closer to that goal. When you arrive at the day when your business is not required to collateralize loans with personal guarantees or your house or boat or whatever you have spent your money on while building your business, you are doing really well and creating multimillion-dollar business success.

By working really hard to establish your business credit you will potentially: 1) Obtain better interest rates and credit terms from banks and lenders. 2) Increase the likelihood of obtaining credit from other businesses. 3) Lower your workers' compensation premiums from insurance companies and 4) Make it easier for business partners to evaluate the risk of doing business with you. But what are you willing to pay to quickly establish creditworthiness in the eyes of potential investors, clients, and other businesses? Think about what you are willing to lose by not taking this proactive step.

When a financial query is done on your firm—and it will be done by serious clients evaluating your ability and financial capacity to deliver—what would you pay to have a great seal of approval? What would it cost you if you had no seal of approval at all? And what would it say to potential clients if you were not savvy enough to even investigate this issue and address how to position your company for financial evaluation? You might look half-baked. You might look like you are not very serious. You might look like you are not a contender and have no business attempting to sell that particular client. Can you afford that scenario? If you are fortunate enough to be considered for a contract with a major firm, the last thing you want or need is for the deal to be derailed because you missed some steps in the planning process. Financial readiness is crucial for any business operation and you should have evaluated the need to appear creditworthy by contacting the financial and business credit builder of your choice. Imagine the confidence you would have coming out of the gate with a fully developed business credit profile. This would quickly establish your firm as a serious operation and may even create some differentiation against your competitors. When all else is equal, whatever advantage you can create can be the winning advantage for you and your firm.

During NobleStrategy's short journey, we have had to sign personal guarantees and pledge personal assets. Currently, my home is not a pledged asset on company financing, however, I have retired several loans where my home was pledged. In the beginning, unfortunately, this may be a common occurrence. As your firm develops, you may be in a position to secure financing with other instruments such as life insurance policies and other cash equivalents.

When we first secured a traditional line of credit in 2008 from a small, local bank, a full three years after working in the firm full time, I was asked to pledge additional collateral for the bank's protection. Even though we had gained multimillion-dollar business success in a short period of time ($2.3 million in gross receipts for fiscal year 2008), we were still required to provide the bank with additional protection. That protection ultimately came in the form of a key man life insurance policy. Key man life insurance can be a great benefit as well as a recruitment and retention tool for your high-profile, skilled employees. It can also ease the collateral requirement for securing a traditional loan since the bank has verifiable proof that, in the event something happens to the key people in that business, their loan will be paid off first from insurance proceeds. We maintain key man life insurance policies for high-level executives to ensure financial capabilities, and can even gain assets on our balance sheet where these policies accumulate cash.

CHAPTER 4 - BOLD MOVES TO MAKE NOW!

✳ Sell your own skills and services part time now by personally doing the work until you can afford to hire staff for your full-time solution.

✳ Evaluate lending alternatives, such as asset-based financing or factoring, when traditional funding is not available.

✳ Quickly establish a business credit profile to successfully migrate away from using your personal credit history.

✳ Utilize community lending resources in the early stages and take advantage of their mandates to assist local businesses.

✳ Get started by using more costly and available funding until you can obtain money at better terms and interest rates.

✳ Don't be afraid to sell to larger businesses, just be prepared for longer payment processes.

CHAPTER 5

TAKE RISKS, HAVE FAITH, AND KEEP PLANTING SEEDS

As you prepare for your entrepreneurial journey, there will be difficulties ahead. Your spirit must be steadfast and your will must be strong. Taking calculated risks is something you will inevitably do on a regular basis but it may, at times, be painful. To ease your pain you need to exercise tremendous faith and have a backup plan. As you begin to evaluate risks that offer greater rewards, potentially *making bold moves* will require you to develop and be constantly supported by your growing faith. You have to develop a confidence and belief that your decisions are sound, wise, and will bear fruit.

Think of the farmer who plants seeds all day, every day. The farmer needs to be focused on making sure the seeds get planted each day. This should be your daily goal as an entrepreneur—to think like the farmer. However, instead of doing as the farmer does by actually planting seeds, you are taking the steps you need to move your business forward. Investing in yourself and "planting seeds" will look more like taking meetings, building relationships, practicing your craft, making investments and perfecting your sales pitch. Although you don't know what kind of fruit your seeds will bear, you plant anyway and keep moving.

That farmer who keeps planting does do a few other things while planting. He gets ready for the harvest through preparation. He doesn't go each day to check on his seeds, he keeps planting and continues to prepare for the harvest, having confidence that good crops will grow. While unsure when or how, you must know that those seeds will grow eventually. What would happen if you planted and coaxed your seeds each day? When harvest comes you might not be ready. You don't always come back to see if the seeds you planted last week are growing, you just trust that they will. When first getting started *you have to be* all about planting seeds. You may get downtime to monitor them every now and again but don't lose focus on planting. Remember, if you have nothing planted, you can expect to harvest nothing in the future. There is no crystal ball in business and you will always wonder how your decisions or investments or partnerships will work out. Have faith in the seeds you plant and decisions you make, keep planting and preparing for the harvest.

Four Critical Meetings

I started planting seeds right away and took the advice of one of my mentors, R.L., who gave me inspiration on time management and prospecting for new business. I was told that I should strive to have at least four meaningful meetings each day—two each morning and two in the afternoon. R.L. also told me to write down every person I met with and recall those names after about six weeks to follow up on any potential opportunities. R.L. said I should repeat that cycle regularly, until I became too busy handling client jobs to continue it. I have to tell you that I was exhausted by doing that.

When I started the firm it seemed that I had a lot of free time so making four meetings a day didn't seem like too much to handle. But when you actually do it, it starts to wear you down. After all, I was in the seed planting stage, waiting for my harvest. Even though I didn't know what fruit those efforts would bear, I set out each day to book four critical meetings. I worked hard to schedule meetings at nine o'clock and eleven o'clock, then in the afternoon at one o'clock and three o'clock. It didn't leave much time for travel or lunch but I worked it out. Folks who saw me prospecting during that period said I was kind of like a superhero, always rushing off with my backpack, prepared for anything, armed with my sales pitch. They dubbed me "Meetingman" and thought it was pretty humorous that I had no actual clients but had meetings all day every day. Those were the seeds I had to plant in order to have a harvest.

It was that discipline, to prospect for meetings each day that turned into my being in the right place at the right time. One of my many morning meetings was with the business development director for a global construction firm. The company was an industry powerhouse with over 46,000 employees worldwide and over 600 in New York City alone. I was able to gain an edge through familiarity with the firm and quickly saw an angle that allowed me to work in an unofficial capacity as an extension of their business development staff. They said, *If you find something out there that we can work on together, bring it to us and let's discuss it.* That was all the incentive I needed. I used my relationships at city agencies to find out where the upcoming projects would be and found a great opportunity that I brought back for discussion. That opportunity became NobleStrategy's first major contract worth over $30 million, with a 30% engagement for our firm, which we won and which turned out to give us our start. The fit was right, the timing was right and I guess I got lucky. However, you must be aware that luck is where preparation and opportunity meet. You have to be prepared, you have to have practiced, and you have to have planted seeds along the way.

Take Risks but Have a Plan B

There will be times when you will have to start making lemonade. Yes, you might need a refreshing drink for your unquenched thirst for success, but if your plan sours and you are left with lemons, hold tight, squeeze hard, stay poised and create a better, sweeter, more satisfying situation.

On a daily basis you will encounter scenarios that will cause you to pause and wonder why you ever thought success could happen for you. Your big decision to quit your job and pursue your dreams will be questioned over and over again. But somehow you will need to keep a determined mind and stay on your path to success in business. Eventually, you will get there, but during the process, your struggle may not be pretty. You will have a great story to tell about how you did it, but it will probably get ugly. As the saying goes: If you've seen sausage made, you probably wouldn't eat it! Once it's done, though, it tastes pretty good. So prepare for the sausage making stage. It *may* not be pretty but it *will* cause you to be a creative, risk-taking force with solid faith and daily encouragement.

You will be required to take risks and, in some cases, you will need to make the best of your resulting situation. Even after developing your faith and preparing for success, you will still need to have your Plan B ready for action. No matter how calculated your risk-taking is, there will be times when the outcome will not be as you planned and you will need a backup plan.

Most business courses discuss planning and implementation in detail but usually focus very little on the Plan B. Your Plan B doesn't have to be a last resort or an alternative where everyone loses. It should be as robust as the initial plan, allowing for multiple wins, market share and advances with your clients. Too often people put so much into developing their initial plan of action that there is nothing left for Plan B.

A good plan, though essential, should always have outlets and options that allow your game-changing idea to move forward in the face of *chaos*. It may mean moving to a fringe market for support during rough times or restructuring your company operations and overhead to support you in a volatile economy. It may also mean having a transition or succession plan in place so that if something happens to you, the entire company doesn't fall apart. People often hear me say, "If I get hit by a bus tomorrow, the show must go on!" Anytime we build a plan, solution, or idea, we have to think about the stability of that plan if a key piece is removed. How strong is your plan if it cannot weather a competitive or transitional storm? If folks who don't usually compete against you lined up for battle in your territory, could you still find a way to win?

MAKE A BOLD MOVE

Strengthen your faith! You will be tested and will need to regularly seek the power you need to keep coming back. Know that you will make it but that you must go through this very necessary process for growth. This won't always be pleasant but it will make your ultimate success story that much more remarkable, and it just may inspire others to travel the path you charted.

Let's suppose your market changed and now there is new competition. And you lose your best people, or customers don't spend like they used to, or agencies are cutting back and the initial plan no longer works. Perhaps you even begin losing market share and revenues. You must find a way to implement your backup plan to combat the effects of the business environment. Conditions like this may not be the norm but your business is operated in the con-text of the current environment and you will need to weather the storms that come. Being prepared for this will require you to take big risks and enact your Plan B, and as long as your plan is robust, it can help you exist and evolve with the market conditions in order to stay in business.

Strengthen Your Faith

During the times business is slow, what will keep you going from day to day? How will you remain encouraged to move forward when the phone is not yet ringing? Where will you turn to strengthen your will and determination to get ahead when the bills are due? The answers may vary but they all contain an essential element: Faith. Believing in the power and spirit of a higher being and the direction that your higher power has for your life will get you through whatever challenges come your way. In everything you do, your prayers and thoughts should be channeled toward increasing your faith to sustain yourself in business.

When I started our firm in 2005, I was immediately faced with having to take huge risks. The first risk required me to leave the comfort of my $118,000-a-year government job and compromise my family and a portion of my savings for my initial investment. I wasn't sure how it would all work out but I did have a plan. I took the leap of faith, knowing that God would not have brought me this far to leave me, and I got started building my dreams. At the time I didn't know when I would return to making enough money to support my family or even match the $118,000 that I walked away from to start the business. But I did believe my pastor who often said, "God has a vision for your life that is greater than any vision you could have or any vision that others could have for you." And I was propelled by that notion. Those words kept me going and helped create the faith and courage I needed to press on. I also learned that what God had for me was for me and couldn't be taken away or disrupted by anyone else. That also meant that what God had for others was not necessarily for me—their blessing was for them and my blessing was for me.

Instead of worrying about whom on a proposal selection committee would or would not vote for me, I leaned on my faith and strong conviction. My faith quickly developed to the point where I knew that if God's plan was for me to have the job, nothing could stop that. And if that was not God's plan, perhaps there was something bigger and better waiting that I couldn't yet see. It becomes difficult to control your desires but your faith will teach you that what you want will come only if it is part of God's plan for you. The challenge is, sometimes you want what you want more than you want to understand what God might have for you. It may not always happen the way you plan, but if you stay faithful it will happen. You will feel like you are constantly being tested, but these will be chances to develop your faith.

Do You Really Want to Succeed?

We can all say that we want to succeed but when faced with making the kind of *bold move* required in a recession, will you take the risk or will you retreat? If you can take fear out of the equation and focus on the facts, outcomes and variables, then you can begin to make clear decisions. You will also need to eliminate the chatter from the talking heads about how bad things are (the business climate, the outlook for entrepreneurs, etc.) in order to calculate your risks. Surrounding yourself with positive people and staying away from negative influences also contributes to your independent decision making and evaluation of opportunities. If you are not strong in your conviction, you can fall prey to folks not making any moves or taking any risks.

I get tired of "herd mentality" thinking—now is not the time to take any chances, hold on to what you have and wait it out. But think of the opportunity and the up side that comes with being able to win big on a calculated risk. After all, nothing ventured, nothing gained. Too many people are immobilized by financial news programs discussing impending doom and gloom in the market. However, building your dream and sustaining your firm's growth will not be supported by fear or herd mentality thinking.

It will take *bold moves* to manage the risks that will afford you the greatest opportunities for success.

- ✓ Develop your skills.
- ✓ Stand on your strengths.
- ✓ Have a Plan B, call on your faith and take risks. Even when your calculated decisions don't yield what you planned there is learning in the recovery.
- ✓ Remember that some lessons are only realized because you remember the pain you felt when you

made the mistake. Either it cost you financially in damages or perhaps you lost a major contract or client. Chances are you will guard against it happening again.

✓ The biggest risk is not moving because of fear. Conquer the fears, calculate the risk and grow your business now!

CHAPTER 5 - BOLD MOVES TO MAKE NOW!

❋ Be prepared to take risks and make bold moves!

❋ Carefully evaluate risk and reward scenarios for each business decision you make.

❋ Once you have made your decision, do the work and start planning for your eventual harvest.

❋ Be aggressive with your time by regularly and consistently scheduling business development meetings for new clients and opportunities.

❋ Develop a thorough Plan "B" and even a Plan "C" to accommodate for things not going the way you originally planned.

❋ As you work, rest on your faith and believe that what the universe has for you is already yours!

❋ Practice what you preach and do the things required each day to move you closer to your goals.

❋ Have faith in your plans but remember that faith will not get you there without hard work.

CHAPTER 6

CREATING WINS FOR THE CLIENT

In order to gain advantage over and differentiation from the competition, you must learn how to adopt a client-win mentality. We can frame the positive attitude required to create client wins on a very large scale right out of the box. Creating wins for the client should be what you are all about at this level. This way of thinking should come through in everything you do. Your main objective here is to develop a winning attitude and create a culture that indicates that your main goal and objective is to create wins for the client. You will be extremely successful at executing this strategy if you can keep the focus on your clients and how your solutions matter to them and for them.

Firms sometimes get caught up in other issues that don't really matter to the client or influence their clients' solutions. Read on to identify success strategies for developing a "win for the client attitude" that will pervade your entire company.

Riding the Wave

Our firm's motto is "A Professional Construction Resource." We believe that if we can create wins for the client, things will work out for us. We don't mind giving the credit to the client once the winning strategy is developed. Sure, we like to hold on to our competitive advantage, but we will gladly let a client take credit for our solution and sometimes our signature materials.

In order to create this culture within your firm, you have to be willing to let your clients "ride the wave" of your success or solution. If you get caught in the headlines trying to grab credit for the solution, how is that a benefit to your client? If your client wins big, there is typically no confusion behind what caused the big win and you will be standing right there for your eventual credit. By allowing your client to harness your situation, brand, or market advantage, you can create a ready-made wave of success that allows the client to ride for free. They don't have to be very well invested in how you arrived at the solution, but if it speaks to their constituents and causes them to win, do everything you can to give them a "ride" and allow them to take the credit.

This is not only effective with large clients but also in building relationships that will be critical to your success. Earlier we discussed the value of political relationships and access. Imagine that you are in a position to highlight the efforts of a local politician to bring jobs to a community. What if you were instrumental in revitalizing a neighborhood by moving your business into a community experiencing renewal? This would surely lend support to the elected official's efforts to revitalize the community or even their taking credit for revitalizing the community.

MAKE A BOLD MOVE

Allow your best clients to ride your wave. Create immediate success for them by utilizing your pre-planned activities and events to address their motives and objectives. Use a promotional event to co-promote a client, cause, or community issue that you can share with your clients, indicating that your wins are their wins, too, and reminding them that you will be a resource for them.

At some point, politicians will be instrumental in providing resources for the businesses and professionals in the community, and if you create a win for them early on, you allow them to ride the wave for their needs, too. If local elected officials are constantly talking about how the neighborhood is changing and taking on a professional appearance in the hopes of luring new businesses, tax payers, and influencers to the area, maybe moving your business into the neighborhood will create a "wave" for that elected official to ride. Would they take the opportunity to speak at your grand opening? Would they be further supported by utilizing the platform you created to bolster their local efforts and initiatives? Would they be glad to know your move allowed them to have more credibility with the community when it came to getting the things done they had committed to? I say yes to all of the above. Furthermore, you will have created access based on the wave you created. Surely, the elected official's door will be open and you will gain immediate access to them. You will be recognized as a contributor and there will be a fast realization that you can assist many efforts through your business leadership. Sounds like a match made in heaven. If nothing else it is at least the beginning of a successful "client-win" strategy that will move you further along on your path to multimillion-dollar success.

We used this concept when we opened our New York office in the community of Harlem in 2009. We knew there weren't many businesses thriving in the recession. We took advantage of that fact and offered our wave for others to ride.

In May of 2009 we were putting the finishing touches on our newly leased 1,700-square-foot space in the first-floor retail portion of a new condominium building on Frederick Douglass Boulevard between 138th and 139th streets. Harlem was undergoing its second renaissance, complete with new housing stock and urban professionals, and the eclectic energy and cultural vibe from this historic community was apparent and attractive. The recession was full blown and there was an alarmingly high rate of unemployment in the community. We prepared a plan that capitalized on the fact that not many businesses were in a position to offer their services to be a resource for the neighborhood. We also knew that the business improvement districts were not really incentivizing folks to relocate to Harlem.

Once we realized the value of being in the community as a leading construction management firm that could influence and assist the neighborhood, we knew we could get people on our side. We cultivated relationships with chambers of commerce and local business alliances, but most importantly with elected officials. Our grand opening was a huge success as we set the stage for folks to ride the wave. Elected officials were able to stand at our podium and proclaim "A new day is here!" They were able to speak with confidence and credibility that here is a well-established firm with enough pride and responsibility to bring business to the community struggling for jobs. We even extended this wave to one of our "big fish" client partners who had a plan to fund almost $2 billion in construction in upper Manhattan and the Bronx.

It took us a while but we had a concept that worked for us and others. Utilizing the resources of our state agency client, we were able to expand the marketing and exposure around our grand opening. Since the event was also to highlight what they were doing, the arrangement was perfect. We co-branded the event and even allowed them to use our tagline, *Making Bold Moves*, which fit right in with the executive director's actions in taking the agency from a traditionally staid focus to aggressively seeking diversity and balance in their procurement processes.

Our wave created the backdrop for our client agency to tell their story and promote their business through our event.

We even coordinated press and promotional efforts to further our reach and send a message loud and clear about what good news was happening and who was at the center of it all. Could we even buy this type of publicity if we had tried? Perhaps not, but our grand opening event offered a meaningful context—a wave—for state agencies to highlight the positive story of job creation where there had not been much good news. It was a nice bonus to also have my picture appear with executive directors of four major city and state agencies that were all able to ride the wave of a successful business, opening at a time when most businesses were closing their doors.

The community benefited from our grand opening as well. We wanted to give a token of our appreciation to all who attended the event but also make a statement. We had the idea to create NobleStrategy lapel pins but quickly realized that, unless you were an employee, you probably wouldn't wear the pin after the grand opening. Then we realized the apparent pride in the Harlem community, which was shared by new and old residents alike. We saw that people quickly proclaimed their allegiance to Harlem. This made us think of a way to capitalize on that spirit and enthusiasm and attach it to our event.

Our concept *Making Bold Moves* again fit the scenario perfectly. Most people from Harlem could identify with *making bold moves* based on the history and culture that existed in this historic community. We also knew that most residents and/or elected officials would be proud to show off their community spirit by wearing a *Making Bold Moves*-Harlem pin. We turned a simple grand opening event into a marketing and exposure campaign to benefit us and the community we would serve. Instantly, we were able to bring attention to Harlem pride and connect it to our firm, a newly integrated Harlem business and institution.

As our elected officials took their press conferences, we knew that getting our *Making Bold Moves*-Harlem pin on them would allow them to demonstrate their Harlem pride but it would also provide a connection to NobleStrategy and our arrival. To this day we still give out the Harlem pin and people still wear it with pride. But they are also promoting our brand, consciousness, and place in the community. We have used *our wave* to successfully mark a period in time with our brand, reminiscent of an unforgettable event for an entire community, inspiring hope and promise during a major recession.

Play With Passion and Change the Paradigm

Your solutions for these clients must be robust and creative in order for you to have success on this level. Passion plays a big role in providing this type of solution because the client needs to know that you really want to be there, working hard for them as opposed to just being satisfied with having a large client on your roster. Passion can be a great differentiator. It can create an opportunity for you to cut through the advantage of firms that have become mainstays with clients over long periods of time. There are many instances where clients receive the same old stale responses to solving their issues. Oftentimes, firms that have long held contracts for big clients seem to assume a complacency that stifles thinking and creativity.

But be careful when you create this new, passion-based model because folks will try to compare you to firms that are not yet thinking like you or producing the results you are. Large agencies tend to draw benchmarks across firms. If they have multiple contracts, they may try to standardize the offering across all firms working. If you have created a new model and have started to shift the paradigm, you will stand out but the accountants will want to know why they should pay more or even the same amount if the other firms are not producing on your level. Either way, your passion will produce for you and your results will stand on their own. You will gain competitive advantage without trying and you will be recognized for your efforts.

MAKE A BOLD MOVE

Use your passion for profits! You might not be the smartest person in the room but you can be the most passionate one in the room about your product, service or experience. Never miss an opportunity to pour your passion into what you do. You will win assignments by virtue of the client making an emotional connection to you based on how strongly you can communicate your willingness to deliver for them, and that is valuable.

Once the paradigm is shifted, folks will start to create contracts that you may have the greatest chance at securing. Based on the results of your current contracts, agencies will look to further detail their outcomes in a new version of what you might be doing already. There won't be frivolous opportunities to win work but real wins. As long as your work is creating wins for your clients, you will be in play and in position to continue to win.

I know from the experiences we have had with some of the largest construction agencies in the New York City area. We have benefited from a paradigm shift caused, in part, by our solutions to client issues. When we win a contract we seek to raise the bar, which can stifle the competition and elevate your game. Once you have established this new benchmark, you will be surprised at how your brand and past performance will begin to create more opportunities. Folks that you previously competed against will now seek you out to join their teams because of your winning reputation.

In 2009 we were working to support a major multimillion-dollar project in New York City for a huge state agency, which required new legislation before the contracts could be issued. Everyone knew the legislation had a great deal of support and would eventually be passed but no one knew when. In an effort to respond to this well-announced request for proposal (RFP), though it was still unfunded and not yet legally possible, we raced to get things in place. We took the risk of putting in all that effort, not knowing whether the legislation would be passed or not. Could we have sat on the sidelines and waited for the legislation before we committed our resources? Yes, we could have but that would not have given us the support or advantage we needed to be seen as a true competitor and a company that could solve the client's needs when they absolutely, positively needed it.

This is another reason why access to local elected officials is critical. Because of these relationships, as we plotted our resources and directed our energy, we were able to eliminate some of our fears and potential risk by having conversations with our elected officials about their confidence in the passing of the legislation.

We jumped in head first and rushed to make ourselves ready and attractive for this upcoming opportunity. These preparations involved months of research and meetings to find the most compelling means of articulating our solution to the "big fish" client. Since this was such a significant opportunity, we partnered with a larger firm to ensure that our team had the full complement of resources, expertise, and local knowledge of the agency that we wanted so badly to go to work for. We quickly developed a comprehensive and creative solution, built on experience, but there was still no legislation passed. After initial submission of our qualifications, we were selected to be one of four firms that would have an opportunity to provide a 30-minute in-depth presentation of their services, but there still was no legislation passed. We waited another three months before the legislation was passed and guess what? Then it was time to move with speed. The client needed so much done in such a short period of time that anyone who had waited to begin preparing their solution would have been decimated trying to meet the agency's quickly approaching deadlines and goals.

Our firm did not win the original contract, but based on the solution we provided and the paradigm shift we created, we were offered a secondary, smaller but still critical contract opportunity. There we were, working as hard as we could to put our team in the winner's circle and lost the major deal. But we were approached by the winner to provide the training solution. They knew we would master the task based on our history and success. At first it seemed hard to explain how and why we were selected and not our partners. But, ultimately, we realized that we were pursued not for what our partners offered but for what we built and branded—emerging contractor mentoring and development. We still pursue the large projects and always chase the multimillion-dollar contracts as prime consultants, but in some cases, working as a sub-consultant to the winning firm is not a bad proposition. What we wanted most was to create a reference for our firm with the agency and we probably would have done the work for free.

Having the opportunity to get in front of major clients and show what you can do is sometimes worth a lot more than you would pay to pursue a contract. We call it offering a commercial when you work for free because you get to leave a lasting impression on the client. You can also learn their processes and build relationships with their managers. This is all very worthwhile, especially if you haven't previously had contact with that agency.

The catch with this particular project was that the entire program had to be up and working within 60 days. This involved a tremendous amount of coordination within both our firm and the firm we were working for. Furthermore, our solution involved us working with about six independent subconsultants and contractors that we were required to coordinate and provide administration for. A huge undertaking by any stretch of the imagination, but the client's goals were clear and they never wavered. The program had to be absolutely up and running within 60 days. We had no contracts, we had no agreements and we had no idea of what we would be paid for our services, but we started the work. If I make the decision to work without a contract, that is my risk; but in this case, I had to convince approximately six other firms to do the same. It was a gargantuan task but we did it and made the client's goals by responding in quick time under less than ideal conditions.

While most any business instructor will tell you not to work on any contract without a signed agreement, sometimes it is just not practical. Depending on the nature of your relationship and the value of your work and credibility with the client, this calculated risk is often mitigated.

In building this contractor training and development plan, we knew the plan had to be robust enough for advanced contractors but also credible enough to hold the interest of the agency's technical and field management staff. We were able to write curriculum, meet with agency officials and construct learning outcomes and objectives that fit the overall goals for the program seemingly overnight. We crunched numbers and stretched the limits of our curriculum development skills to satisfy the goals. It was a tall task but we made it happen because we knew if we caused the client to win, ultimately we would put ourselves in a very good place.

We selected top-notch professionals to teach and then built solid core goals, objectives and materials into the program. The program was successful—the client got what they needed and we branded another "big fish" client strategy that we are very proud of on a contract we still hold today. It took us another 90 days after the program started before we received our agreements and contracts, but we created a win for the client and that was very valuable. Not only did we get paid for a robust solution that worked, we also branded our company in the client's mind by getting the virtually impossible done in a very short period of time.

This was not our first "big fish" client and our expertise and knowledge of how to work with this type of client contributed to our success. We shifted the paradigm and caused the competition to have to do the impossible just for a chance to match us. We knew what to look for, what could happen and what not to worry about. Did we take risks? Yes, we did. Did we protect ourselves? Yes, we did. Did we go out on a limb for the client? Yes, we did. Were we successful? Yes, we were. Would we do it again? Yes, we would. Once the tide has turned and the paradigm has shifted, your clients will know what to expect from you and how valuable your solutions are. You can instantly level the playing field and even gain a competitive edge dealing on your own terms once you have raised the bar with your calculated risk-taking. Any opportunity for you to win for a major client could turn into a potential long-term agreement that can be used to further your advantage against the competition and build your firm's revenues. Take that risk every chance you get and commit to *making bold moves* for your clients.

Clients Can Create Wins for You Too

When I talk to savvy business owners, I always encourage them to build relationships with agency firms and create references for their firms, even if they work in low-bid environments. There is always an opportunity where an agency director needs assistance or is in a position to advise a winning contractor on achieving their diversity goals. Agency personnel who know your firm can, and sometimes will, suggest that the major players talk to minority- and women-owned businesses (M/WBEs). Surprisingly, a deal can be done just like that. This is a good strategy not only for firms looking to build revenue but also for firms seeking to position themselves for upcoming contracts. Even in our business where teaming is a favorable concept, we will often inquire—off the record—about firms that are familiar to an agency and might have stellar reputations, in the hopes of having that strength on our team for a win.

There are only a few agencies that I could credit with being very serious about minority- and women-owned businesses on the city and/or state level, but we are always hopeful that more will emerge. These agencies are very interested in creating wins for you and your firms and work very hard to push new initiatives and enforce existing regulations to ensure participation. These agencies have demonstrated a strong and continuous commitment to growing M/WBEs and are extremely serious about achieving their goals for diversity.

Over the last several years, firms have benefited from the industry champions who lead these agencies that advocate regularly for the inclusion and growth of minority firms. One particular agency I know of has supported and sustained a culture that has made their programs nationally recognized models of success, and their efforts have been well-preserved by one of the best executive leadership teams in the city. If you speak to any of these individuals about their assistance in developing new firms across the city, you might be amazed at their level of accessibility and commitment to the challenge of inclusion and diversity in agency procurement and, most specifically, construction projects across the city of New York.

I also know of agencies that have not had a stellar record of diversity in the past but are quickly making up for lost time. One great thing about the emergence of the new programs is that they seek to increase business for not only M/WBEs but also disadvantaged business enterprise (DBE) firms, since they receive a mix of state and federal funds on projects. Some of their projects require DBE goals of at least 20% while other projects require goals to ensure the use of M/WBE firms across all procurement. With the agency's addition of a few key executives and a commitment to change the culture, they can quickly ramp up and be taken seriously. In establishing new small business development programs, complete with access to new contract opportunities for M/W/DBEs, there are now many more agencies open for business throughout the state for firms who previously had no real chance to work in those environments. They are increasing their diversity spend while adequately balancing state and federal tax payer funds to spur economic activity in all communities, which is not just noble but necessary.

Get to know the industry champions who are willing to support businesses like yours and who can advocate for your collective industry issues. Leverage their efforts to build momentum to keep your goals in view as you pursue opportunities in public agencies through diversity and inclusion means. Being the best you can be and adopting a "client must win" attitude will add dollars to your revenue and improve your retention rate on existing customers. And it will allow your clients to become brand ambassadors wherever possible, ultimately creating a couple of wins for you, too.

CHAPTER 6 - BOLD MOVES TO MAKE NOW!

* Be creative and build solutions that ultimately create wins for your clients!

* Use your passion as a key differentiator to propel you into an uncontested market and cause separation from the pack of competitors.

* Find your competitive advantage over others and exploit it at each opportunity, all the while leveraging the end results for your clients.

* Work for free now but quickly show your value and willingness to deliver and turn that unpaid assignment into an extensive, well-paid client relationship.

* Offer solutions that can support the client and the community, increasing the value of your contribution.

* Don't be afraid to give your clients the credit for the job, and remember that as long as they win, so do you!

* Get to know the industry champions in your field and understand their motivation and concerns in order to create a "win" for them.

CHAPTER 7

PITCHING THE PRIMES

One very important aspect of early business success for our firm was our ability to work in conjunction with very large prime contractors. A prime contractor is a lead contractor or consultant working in a primary capacity on a contract, often engaging smaller contractors or sub-consultants to complete the work. There is no doubt that certain rules and restrictions for working with megafirms exist and we have worked to master those requirements. In actuality, when larger primes are pursuing certain projects, they may need us more than we need them. They won't usually let on to that fact, but not getting the minority business enterprise (MBE) aspect of the project correct could mean losing millions of potential dollars in opportunities. Moreover, for these large firms, it can cost from $25,000 to $40,000 preparing an RFP response and no one wants to sacrifice that kind of cash. When you are stacked against the fiercest competitors in the industry, especially during recessionary times, every step has to be calculated. No one wants to spend weeks coordinating hours and preparing a response without hitting the mark quickly on all the aspects you can control.

Selecting the right partners, sub-consultants or team players will ultimately be an important deciding factor, and even the megafirms—firms that have been in existence for nearly 100 years that control market share and major revenue—sometimes get it wrong. For the firms that don't understand this aspect of the business, survival can become a difficult task. I have even seen instances where a large firm is battling with the client at the RFP interview presentation table because they didn't take the M/WBE aspect seriously. Their lack of planning and sensitivity really communicated that either they are not interested in supporting M/WBEs or don't understand how or why the M/WBE firms can contribute to their success.

We had a chance to participate in preparing an RFP response for a $300 million design build project in Harlem. We did our research, joined community task forces, and represented our firm and issues well. We worked and campaigned for about one year to get on the right team and we finally succeeded in securing a spot on an internationally recognized leader's team. We were selected as one of five firms to offer a 60-minute presentation on our team approach and value. We did even more research, learned all aspects of the community demographics and prepared to lead convincing arguments for outreach and workforce development issues connected to the project.

We rehearsed for about four days but, unfortunately, the firm we partnered with had devoted only about five minutes of their 60-minute presentation to those very critical community issues. In addition we learned that a competing firm that was also required to give a 60-minute presentation did not include any of the community aspects or the value of coordination of M/WBE activities in their plan for discussion. Yes, folks, even with the record number of minority businesses across this nation (over 1.2 million black businesses with gross revenues of over $88 billion in 2002 according to the U.S. Census Bureau) and with our contributions rising, we were about to initiate a project worth a potential $300 million without a major discussion focused on MBEs.

Our nation has seen a great emergence and call for diversity and change—as evidenced by the first African American President, Barack Obama—so why would this large firm not think diversity would be critically important to their chances of winning the contract? There are very smart, resource-loaded firms still getting the diversity discussion wrong every day and it's very surprising.

In early 2011 an international megafirm settled a criminal investigation for $20 million but admitted no wrongdoing. The issue was that they had worked with an MBE firm that was, allegedly, a minority front, defrauding public agencies and other firms out of millions of dollars in contract opportunities. I'm not sure how or why this continues to happen but, with all the advances we have made, some folks are not interested in changing the way they do business.

On July 15, 2010, New York's Governor David Paterson signed into law the Business Diversification Act of 2010. While the signing of this Act into law was historic and gave New York— the financial capital of the world—stronger legislation to ensure participation across all state agencies, it only happened recently. I was very glad to see the legislation and hopeful that these laws would be vigilantly enforced to create the culture required to grow and sustain New York's M/WBE community. In fact, the groundbreaking legislation—part of the M/WBE Business Diversification Act of 2010, which was considered a victory for the M/WBE community as well as the state of New York—is comprised of Governors Program Bills 297, 298, and 299 and the Emerging Investment Managers Bill. The legislation that created the Business Diversification Act of 2010 enacted by Gov. Paterson, which was adopted on December 22, 2010, is extremely critical and necessary to grow capacity and extend opportunities to minority- and women-owned businesses, which will further activate a previously stagnant economy. It is also our hope that this legislation delivers on the promise to build capacity through increased business opportunities for qualified M/WBE firms deserving of a fair and level playing field on which to compete in New York State.

When you do get a chance to partner with firms who truly "get it" and are not just doing it because it's the law, you can build long, lasting relationships. We have formed a few of these relationships, which have proven to be very valuable in achieving our desired growth goals. While all of these relationships have been critical in our growth, key deals have also offered our partner firms a great value as well. When you can continually make the relationship a two-way street, no one feels compelled to continue to work with you. In most cases, when the value goes, so, too, will the partner firm and relationship.

Interestingly enough, megafirms usually all want the same thing: exclusivity! At first it bothered me a little that with such huge opportunities available to them they would seek to restrict potential opportunities for smaller firms, but it is all about being competitive, adding value, and creating differentiation. I quickly came to understand the need for exclusivity and even utilize the practice myself when we pursue projects as a prime with an assembled team.

Our relationship with our current partners has provided major opportunities for growth since we started in 2005. These relationships and opportunities also have to continually evolve to satisfy each partner's needs. Initially, we set out to automatically market our firm as a true, joint venture partner with other firms but that didn't always work. Even though we might not have had the record, balance sheet or business acumen early on for the joint venture, I pressed the issue because we had to ultimately get there. And, I thought, like most firms who start out, *why wait when we wanted it now!*

Two of my fondest work periods came early in my career and involved me being exposed to joint ventures that worked, and they fueled my fire to start my own business. In 1990, upon graduating from Hampton University with a BS in Building Construction Technology, I was recruited to work in Harlem, New York for a growing MBE. The Firm was run by a shrewd businessman who I often credit with sparking my business interest and success. While at The Firm, I was exposed to various MBE advocacy programs and organizations that provided training, business networking, and community support. I quickly learned the importance of growing a qualified MBE enterprise and how lucrative it could be from what the owner of The Firm had built. At their peak in 1998, The Firm had revenue of approximately $50 million and was responsible for building several major projects in the New York City market. I witnessed firsthand how building great associations and partnering with large majority firms could grow your venture.

Two very notable projects I was exposed to were the $30 million Schomburg Center for Research in Black Culture and the $100 million Kings County Hospital Renovations. Shortly after my stint with The Firm, I was hired away for less than a $2,000-a-year salary increase to work for yet another MBE construction management firm. This was a family-run father and son team who partnered with large majority firms for immediate success. To this day I am grateful and very fortunate for the contributions they were able to make in the market and to my career.

As I mentioned, I was hired away for less than $2,000 more than I was already making. It was 1990 and I was making $30,000 a year as a young, aspiring project manager. Many folks would not leave a job and major opportunities for growth for only $2,000, but at 21 and wanting it all, the extra $2,000 was my way to the top. Thinking I had "arrived" I was often brought back down to earth when walking the construction site with my clipboard. Managing just a small aspect of the project, I often came upon guys working "in the hole" as electricians making $60 to $70 an hour while I was actually only making the equivalent of about $16 an hour. I was young and ignorant but stayed up and learned quickly. Still no success overnight.

At the second firm, I worked on several joint venture projects that created my expertise and helped me developed a great perspective on joint ventures, partnerships and sub-consulting agreements.

NobleStrategy's first large opportunity came in 2005 when we learned of a potential contract at one of New York City's largest agencies (worth between $30 and $50 million). With my new reputation intact, I hoped that by networking and keeping my ear to the streets I might learn a new business angle or information that could assist our pursuit. Part of my sales strategy early on was to create exposure for myself and stay visible at industry events in order to stay in tune with the environment and learn information on opportunities. Through our research, we learned that several large majority firms would also be pursuing this work but needed a differentiation strategy since they had not won the contract previously.

We pursued discussions with two of the leading firms in the CM arena where we had key relationships from the past with top executives from each firm. We knew we would get our meetings and, if we could put enough value on the table, we might have a shot at being the sole sub-consultant for their teams.

Corporation "A" was a leading provider of engineering, construction and technical services for public agencies and private sector companies around the world. They offer a full range of program management: planning, design and engineering; systems engineering and technical assistance; construction and construction management; operations and maintenance; decommissioning and closure services for power, infrastructure, industrial and commercial businesses; and federal projects and programs.

Corporation "B" was a leading, award-winning professional firm offering engineering, architectural planning, and environmental and construction management services. They consistently rank among the country's top 25 firms in education, highways, bridges, rail and mass transit. Throughout the United States, their 1,700 professional, technical and support personnel offer services to a broad and ever-expanding client base. They provide planning, environmental design; program and construction management and specialty services for the transportation, design-build, institutional and commercial building, advanced technology, industrial, and defense markets.

While both firms had a tremendous national profile with many key sectors to operate within, the New York City K-12 schools market was a major pursuit for each of them. Although Corporation "A" had a large international base with over 45,000 employees, to their credit approximately 600 of them were in the New York City area. Corporation "B" on the other hand was not as large and did not have an international footprint, but they had been recognized for years as a major player in the New York City market. Despite the size and magnitude of both of their operations compared to ours, we had value to offer them as a local, qualified minority business enterprise. Anyone responding to the RFP would be required to offer strong MBE involvement as part of their team for consideration, and they both knew my reputation and what we had set out to start as a company.

Make the Pitch and Make It Happen

With no formal employees and nothing more than a few great concepts, a willingness to over-deliver, and a passion to create wins, I started to perfect my pitch to each of the firms. I quickly learned that they were interested but both firms immediately asked for exclusivity on the pursuit. I was at a crossroads. From the beginning I wanted to play the percentages and knew our chances of being on the winning team would be improved with two shots at the target instead of one.

From my days working at other government agencies in New Jersey where I served on selection committees, I often saw the same M/WBE firms in high demand on several proposing teams. When I realized M/WBE firms could work on multiple teams, I knew that those firms were either very good at what they did and could bring value or that there were not many qualified M/WBE firms out there for large firms to partner with. Or perhaps it was a combination of the two. With that clear understanding, I tried to negotiate to be on both teams simultaneously and quickly learned that it would be next to impossible to pull it off in the New York market. Nonetheless, I presented our value to each firm and evaluated the proposed pursuit deals on their merit.

Initially I was offered a spot as the MBE sub-consultant on Corporation "A"s team with a 15% scope of work. I knew we didn't want to be window dressing and just along for the ride. We wanted to make a real contribution. We knew that being able to make a real contribution would be necessary to grow our firm the way we wanted to and to get recognition for the value we were able to bring to our partners and our clients. Corporation "B" then countered

MAKE A BOLD MOVE

Negotiate the unexpected! No one expects you to ask for much as a start-up but don't be afraid to push the envelope. Do your research, study your clients and find your value proposition, then exploit it for the best scenario you can create based on their weaknesses and your strengths. You should be prepared to ask for anything you want, no matter how ridiculous. If the timing or circumstances are right, you just might get a "yes!"

with an offer of 20% to join their team. I knew that, with them, I wanted a real opportunity to build a lasting relationship, more than I wanted a couple more percentage points on the deal. I had to evaluate which firm would be the best partner, offer the best terms and give us the best opportunity to grow. I had come to the point where no one wanted to discuss anything other than exclusivity, and I had to make a final decision.

The $30 million RFP was just a couple of weeks away and I was pressed to give my decision to both firms. When negotiating with Corporation "B," however, I got the feeling that I would not be the primary sub-consultant but that they would reach for additional horsepower by bringing in another MBE firm larger than ours. I didn't want to play in second position even though I really had no track record. I stood up for what I thought I should have.

I wrestled with the decision for the remaining weeks leading up to the RFP release. I weighed pros and cons and assessed the situation each way I could think of to try to arrive at a decision. I was able to comfortably negotiate a better deal and decided to pursue exclusivity with Corporation "A," with which I felt we'd make a real contribution and add real value. Of course, the firm that you decide not to pursue the deal with may not be happy since so much effort is put into creating the right team from the start. I did inform Corporation "B" that I would not pursue the deal with them and even assisted them in finding someone (a friend of mine) who had just started her own firm, a woman-owned business enterprise (WBE) construction manager. Incidentally, she is still working with them on the assignment they won at the agency and we often share stories and strategies in our current work assignments as the agency performs their standardization and benchmarking across firms.

I made my pitch, worked feverishly on the RFP and we won our first major deal valued at approximately $30 million with Corporation "A." Oddly enough, Corporation "B" also won a $30 million contract during the proposal stage, but there was no way I could have been on both teams at the time of submission. Since then, we have built a great relationship with Corporation "A" based on our mutual respect, passion and knowledge of how to support large firms on these types of projects. We have gone on to four more major contracts at the agency and have also completed projects with them in Miami, Florida. To date we have completed or are currently participating in over $200 million in projects with our current partner, and it's still a wonderful partnership both for us and our clients. We have found a niche in pitching the primes to complement their teams on multi-million-dollar pursuits where they value the passion we bring or need an edge that comes with hiring an emerging firm. We think differently and are less encumbered by our size, tradition or culture. We can take calculated risks and be creative where other firms may not have the opportunity to do so.

In pitching the primes during your initial days, be ready to *make a bold move* and identify details of how you can assist a firm that is probably 10 times your size with value, passion and creativity. Don't be afraid to utilize your advantage and a bit of the "judo principle"—where your relative small size is an asset and their very large size and culture a liability. Practicing this principle affords you the chance to use their size against them and immediately show them how your passion and nimbleness can work in their favor. Get strategic, find the value proposition, meet the needs and partner with a well-established, large majority firm to accelerate your path to business success.

CHAPTER 7 - BOLD MOVES TO MAKE NOW!

* Uncover new markets by finding firms larger than yours to sell services to and support in their goals.

* Whether your work is proven or not, ask for anything in the negotiations because they just might say *Yes!*

* Use your leverage in a regional or local market to gain a clear advantage in teaming up with prime firms when pursuing a critical proposal.

* Bring creative solutions to the table since you might have a better perspective and more passion than the large firm you team up with.

* Discuss options with more than one large prime firm at a time for a comparative analysis of each offer and more leverage.

* Increase your chances of being on the winning team by holding discussions with more than one firm.

* Create demand for your services by researching a new opportunity that larger firms in your market may be interested in to support a "win."

* Identify the largest firms in your market and the specific challenges they face in a region or with a client so you can immediately add value by offering the right solution.

* If faced with offering exclusivity to a large partner in a major pursuit, evaluate the best offer and make the deal.

CHAPTER 8

LANDING THE "BIG FISH" CLIENT

Of all the compelling lessons and tips you can use from this book, the one that is most likely to guarantee your immediate success is landing a "big fish" client. I'm sure most businesses feel that landing the big client will put them over the top, but there is a science to researching and studying "big fish" targets as well as creating the right opportunity to land them. Most of all, you have to devote time, energy and passion to being in position to respond when they call, once you finally get on their radar. The steps outlined herein will take you through the process of getting on their radar, preparing for and seizing the moment to perform extraordinarily for the "big fish" client. It is these recipes that will get you noticed and give you the opportunity to move your business out of your home or your head and into a prominent position in the market.

Before I discuss the how, where and what to do to land the big fish, I'd like to talk about the why. Why is it so important to land a "big fish" client? Several reasons come to mind, including the ability to be seen as a true competitor by folks in the industry. Another is to be at the striking point of new developments spurred by the "big fish" client outcome. Next is the opportunity to market the solutions you built on a very large scale to clients that are smaller than your "big fish" clients. No doubt there will be tremendous respect and credibility attached to the wins you can create for a large client, and given the opportunity to gain those kinds of powerful solutions, smaller clients will jump at the chance to work with you.

Appearing on Their Radar

Before you can sell to the largest clients, you need to appear on their radar. If you are selling services to public agencies or municipal governments, big clients or even Fortune 500 companies, one of the first opportunities to show up on their radar is to be a certified minority-owned or women-owned business (M/WBE).

MAKE A BOLD MOVE

Master the paperwork. The documentation process for getting certified can be daunting but it usually doesn't change. Learn it once and develop a system to stay well versed in maintaining your ultimate edge. Stack your shelves neatly with tax returns, financial statements and updated interim balance sheets so that when they are requested, you easily pass those initial screens often used to separate the more committed firms from their less motivated counterparts.

Business owners sometimes miss the impact that these certifications can offer, just to get you in the game. Typically, the process of certifying your firm will require a few forms and appending tax, corporate ownership, and financial documents to your submission. At the very least, you can expect to be required to submit two years of previous business tax returns, two years of previous personal tax returns, stock registers, corporate resolutions, bank resolutions, articles of incorporation and documents certifying your identity and initial contributions for ownership of the company. Even though this process is straightforward, many businesses succumb to the pressures of pulling together all the required information necessary while trying to market themselves and make money, too. And even though you can prove that you are the majority owner of one of the accepted minority classes or genders, you are still required to maintain and renew these certifications every two to three years.

As a certified minority or woman business enterprise (MBE or WBE), where a protected ethnic or gender group owning at least 51% of a business can obtain a state, city or agency-specific certification, your certification may create your opportunity for a contract. Even having a designation of disadvantaged business enterprise (DBE), which is used on federal transportation projects, allows you to have a leg up when competing for specific contracts. Of course, this certification is a bit of a misnomer since disadvantaged means that your personal net worth, excluding your personal home, is less than $750,000. I know many business owners who would not consider themselves disadvantaged in a traditional sense, but the law allows for the designation based on your net worth.

When transitioning from employee to entrepreneur, you might find getting this certification worthwhile since a lot of professionals in today's economy struggle to gain a positive net worth. But based on the U.S. Department of Transportation and their designation, you can maintain a positive net worth of up to $750,000 and have aggregate revenues of $23 million before you lose this designation. I know this doesn't sound like your typical disadvantaged business (with aggregate revenues of $23 million) but I don't make the rules. Learn this system and find ways to allow these laws and provisions to further develop your business model and strategic plan for growth.

Surely, you won't win work or build a very profitable business if you are only marketing your minority or disadvantaged business status, but if you use it as a means of showing up on their radar, at least you are now in the conversation. Many large private clients and municipal governments are required to diversify their procurement spending. Whether they are purchasing janitorial services, or manufactured building systems or subway cars, it is to their advantage to be able to at least have certified M/WBEs or even DBEs as part of their procurement process. Large firms and government agencies often gain credit for reaching goals set by their boards or, in some cases, local governments that require them to be inclusive of local and minority businesses as they conduct their business. There are even instances where agencies can cause contractors financial hardship if they have not appropriately complied with the law requiring them to do business with minority firms.

If you are selling services to government agencies, you will want to follow procurement legislation and diversity rules concerning your industry and region of operation. When former Governor David A. Paterson signed into law the Business Diversification Act of 2010, among other things it required all New York state agencies to increase their spending with minority- and women-owned businesses. Since most of the funding these agencies receive is comprised of taxpayer dollars, it is imperative that the legislation reflects balance and diversity in its procurement practices. Even if you are selling to private businesses, they will want to associate themselves with diverse and competitive procurement practices and will look to gain credit from working with these certified businesses. Associations like the National Minority Supplier Diversity Council are great leads into private companies looking to do business with minority- and women-owned firms. It is better to go where the firms are that want to do business with M/WBEs than to try to uncover and co-opt corporations who currently don't have any record of or commitment to diversity. This does not mean, however, that they will not be potential targets once they recognize that their competitors are faring better because of the increased competition they have been able to spark. Furthermore, when the legislators start to ask questions or an incident creates public pressure, companies who have not invested in diversity often scramble to make things better. It helps if you are in position with your quality services and products, as well as your certifications, to assist them in diversifying their practices. Let's face it—you are working to be a resource for these "big fish" clients, so whatever you can do to help them and their process will cause you to win in the long run.

Preparing for the Right Moment

One of the things that I've noticed and hope more firms will take notice of is the level of preparation required to sell to large clients. If you know you have dreams of growing your firm, then you have to start to think about how and what it looks like to sell to firms who buy huge amounts of services or products. Being able to balance the many parts of your internal operations—such as finance, production, sales, research and legal concerns—will determine if you are ready to sell on the next level. This is the time when you will be forced to spend more energy on the flow of your internal operations than on the big idea that you want to use to get to the large clients.

Examine your current staff and audit your resources. If you hit it big with a big fish tomorrow, are you ready? Evaluate the health of your business on the key areas that have to be harnessed for "big fish" clients, such as cash/credit, staff, production, legal concerns and sales. Ask yourself—can my current staff execute on my great ideas if they are picked up by a large client? Will my access to capital allow me to advance my operation and deliver for the client that probably has a payment cycle that lasts more than 90 or 120 days? Should my sales team have access to customer relations management software to track leads and keep up with new business developments once I become consumed by this new big fish? Would my "big fish" client buy more services if my technical staff's credentials were enhanced?

Each one of these questions may represent an area of investment required for you to move to the level where you can land a big fish. You have to ask yourself these questions to make sure that, when you do try to land the big fish, you don't drop your line into a pool of man-eating piranhas. If you find that you don't have all you need, then you know exactly where to start to shore up your operation to maintain the foundation that will grow your future success once the big fish is in the net. False moves in this territory will rip you apart and cause you to lose valuable time sustaining your market position and concepts in the industry, not to mention provide a storybook ending for your competitors.

If you are manufacturing belts and making them by hand locally but have the opportunity to get in front of a "big fish" client that may order 20,000 or 30,000 belts as a small order, you have to have invested in the systems required to scale up to that type of production. It may mean you have to investigate production facilities overseas or licensing agreements to make sure— once you land the big fish— that you can ship the goods. You may even have

MAKE A BOLD MOVE

When absolutely necessary, turn up the heat on the "big fish" clients to remind them of your value when you are not getting paid. While you should have an alternative for existing without their immediate payment, don't be afraid to advise them that you may lose the capability to continue services if there is no one willing to advocate for your being paid in a timely manner (within 60 days).

to research more affordable production costs because, on orders that large, they will surely want you to drop your prices. Perhaps you were only making a small margin selling locally because of the costs of goods sold. Well, if you have plans of scaling your operation up, you should know that those resources won't be adequate for you taking your operation to the "big fish" client if you can't make enough money to support the price point at which they want to purchase.

Financing is also key on this level because, most of the time, you won't be able to convince your "big fish" client to pay you like, perhaps, some of your smaller clients do. For large agencies and Fortune 500 firms, the payment process is highly automated and works without personal interaction. The payment chain should be able to hum along very efficiently without the constant provoking of managers "walking payments through the system." So if checks are signed and printed every month and processing takes 30 days, you must be prepared to provide your products and or services to the client without the expectation of receiving payment for at least 60 days. If the payment process is less efficient, it may require 90 to 120 days before payment is made available. In such a case, could you even perform if you weren't paid for three to four months? You have to consider what happens. I know because I have been on both sides of the scenario and have had to consider what to do when a client has not paid me for up to four months.

One of the ways our firm used to combat this issue was by utilizing the services of an accounts receivable factoring company. As mentioned in Chapter 4: Getting Paid Now and More Later, this may be a means of freeing you up so you are not waiting on your money. But this may also be very expensive. Even though you strive to build personal relationships with clients, you must also make sure they value your services. We worked for a city agency that had a very large process and our getting paid was contingent on the state making grant payments to the city we worked for. The agency had no money to pay us on their own but could always guarantee that once they received their payment, they would pay us.

In this case we were subject to two very long government payment processes. We had to wait for their total requisition to be submitted to the state, and then await payment and processing of requisitions that were handled directly by the city agency. There was a period when we were out 120 days, waiting for payment, and had to contemplate suspending our services to the client. In our case, it wasn't because we couldn't afford to pay our workers; it was that we felt that if we did not force the issue of value for the client, who knows how they would proceed in the future.

We felt the need to get their attention by advising them that if they could not make sure we got paid in a timely manner, we would have to suspend our services. "We can no longer afford to show up each day and work on your behalf if there is not much effort and value put into securing payment for our services," I said. There are not many times that you can push your "big fish" clients but this was a case where we thought it necessary to take a step in the affirmative to seek consistent payment. It worked for us in this case.

We quickly met with the city administrator and they recognized that there was a pressing issue to resolve. If nothing else, it shed light on a process that was supposed to work better than it was actually working. Not only did we get our payment within two weeks of that meeting but we also gained a commitment from the city to project the remaining payments and cash flow so we would know the timing of the process and how it should work under normal circumstances.

Seizing the Moment

If you have tirelessly prepared yourself for the right moment and have worked to appear on the radar of the larger clients, you must wait for the right time and seize your moment with a dynamic winning situation for the client. While timing plays a major role in having the large client's needs match up with what you can provide, your preparation is what will make the deal possible. Think of the instances where a major firm has a role to fill or creates an opening in their once seemingly impenetrable exterior and they have a great deal of trouble filling their needs. As hard as it is to sell to these clients, they do have moments when their purchasing is adapted to specific or narrowly focused needs, such as specialty services, or they are required to respond to the increased call to diversify their spending. No matter what creates the opportunity or opening in the procurement process, your chances to win are greatly enhanced by a *rapid response mentality, the ability to provide creative solutions and making sure your clients win with your passion.*

Response, Creativity and Passion

Although working with "big fish" clients sometimes seems bureaucratic and slow, things do get done. The pace and velocity of work is much greater on the consultant side than it is on the client side. You are expected to produce on a level several times greater than the level at which the client or institution might be working. After all, if they didn't have you as a lever to accelerate the pace of the work, why would they need you at all? This type of environment requires well-thought out but timely solutions, often in a very short time frame. Are you at all familiar with the saying: *When they say jump, we say, 'How high?'* If so, then you are starting to prepare to work on the big fish level. You will be asked to provide solutions with very little information and sometimes conflicting departmental goals. However, your charge is to make sense of it all, coordinate the competing interests and deliver the product in an accelerated manner. It sounds difficult and it is but, once again, if it wasn't, they would have no need for you at all. Be sure you can gear up your operation for quick deployments and faster results.

As I mentioned in Chapter 6: Creating Wins for the Client, often, in order to meet the deadlines demanded, you might have to work in less than optimal conditions or even without contractual agreements. We always advise firms not to work until they have directions and or contracts executed in writing but, realistically, that is not always feasible. You will be asked to evaluate the risk associated with executing without a contract. Depending on your client and what is at stake, waiting for your fully executed agreement before you start the work process may kill the project altogether and sink the champion "big fish" client you are trying to support. When working on this level you quickly see the relationship of big causes and legislation to big fish and agency clients. You must think of yourself as a resource for the client to assist them in getting things done. If you approach the project as finally having arrived and are ready to grab your windfall from the big fish, it will never work. You must buy in to the concept that your success is their success, and that is the only way you will continue your existence swimming in the big pond with the big fish.

Don't be afraid to show your passion for the project and/or client. Folks always respond well to passionate deliveries and people want to know that the people they pay to do their work want to be there. Believe it or not, I still find consultants who, in more ways than one, tell their clients they have other things they could be doing. Imagine if you were managing a multimillion-dollar public agency or even a local nonprofit with major construction projects and you have to deal with professionals who don't think you are important. I have had the pleasure of working on the other side in a previous life and can tell you that you need to know the people you hire really want to be there. You need to quickly learn to govern with passion and manage every opportunity to have your work product speak for itself. You can always amplify your brand and tell your story, but the effort you put in and the attitude your people bring to the project will say the most and usually tell everything the client wants to hear.

In January of 2006 our firm won our first major contract at a leading construction agency. Although we were merely a sub-consultant on the contract, we had landed a big fish and were on our way to creating wins for the client. This was a major deal since the contract was worth approximately $30 million. We negotiated a 30% role and scope of services and quickly made a great impact on the client by creating wins for our construction partner as well as the agency. We knew the power of giving credibility to a project executive's decision to bring our minority firm in to help win the contract could not be understated. Our approach was so vastly different from the competitors that we believe it enabled us to gain a favorable position with our partner firm to offer differentiation. We have maintained this relationship since 2006 and are still winning contracts together. We think they have a great group of professionals and they like our work staff as well, but the relationship only lasts because of mutually beneficial value and attitude we bring to continue creating wins for the clients. They feel our passion and allow us the creativity, freedom and even autonomy to make decisions both on their behalf and together as partners. While a sub-consultant having a 30% engagement in a contract is nothing new, the unique position occurred when, upon winning the next contract valued at $100 million, the client asked me to be the project manager.

There were project managers with perhaps more experience than I, but I don't think they had as much passion as I did. Our partners submitted two project managers and the client passed on them both. After their third highly-regarded project manager was on the job for several months, the client still wasn't satisfied. They immediately asked, What about Bill? I thought there would be no way, as president of a growing firm, that I could also manage the position of project manager on such a large contract. With so many other tasks seemingly undone I cringed at their initial request and said no. I really didn't think it would be the

MAKE A BOLD MOVE

Be the project manager! Although you are at the top of the executive suite, don't be afraid to communicate to your clients how important they are to you. Take the challenge of personally delivering the solution for your most important clients. It will be a real opportunity to show your passion for the project and it clearly suggests to the client that they are a priority and that you want them as a client forever! This also gives you a chance to say it as well.

best situation for me or the business at that time. I knew it would require me to attend more meetings on site and visit schools in the field, as well as manage the 30-person staff we had at the time.

Though my concerns may have been valid, initially I was only thinking of myself and how I would be affected. After the second request to have me inserted as the project manager I realized I could not refuse. If you are going to be in the business of creating wins for clients, first you have to be responsive to your clients. You have to be in a position to listen and respond to what they need. My initial refusal didn't do that, it only served me. Once I realized what they were saying, I realized that not only was it a great opportunity to create a win for the client but there was no way I could say no. After all, the longevity of our firm and our contract with the agency was on the line.

I quickly adopted the mentality—which would propel me with confidence and faith as the project manager for the entire team—that wins would be created for the client. Our partners were the prime on the contract but I was listed as the project manager and served in that capacity. I had worked in state and municipal government for several years, dating back to 1990, and I had never seen that scenario—where the minority partner takes lead as project manager on a contract. I said yes but asked for a couple of provisions that would support our field management and staffing needs, then began major efforts to create wins for this very important client.

That period was extremely difficult but it worked. And I say, even to this day, that this client is a client I want to have forever. And forever, as you know, is a very long time. Leading the team as project manager meant preparing documents and doing research on each and every contract and contractor in the program. The folks who manage the agency are all very sharp and focused on what they do so if you are not as focused, it will show right away and they will dispose of you quickly. You could be queried at any time and it can be very embarrassing if you are in your weekly project management meeting with eight other executives and a question is raised and you are unprepared. In order to prevent being embarrassed, you must prepare frantically to stay ahead of the client. After all, they think, since they are paying you to be in front, that you should always know more about the projects than they do, and they are absolutely right.

I am still taxed by the exhaustive demands of the agency and our staff, but I would not have it any other way. I know, at the end of the day, that I am solely responsible and in a position to create wins for this client, and that I have the resources and staff to make it happen.

In 2007, the wins we created for our client were returned in the form of accolades and recognition. Our team won a coveted Construction Manager of the Year award for the breakthrough performance and efforts we supplied during our initial years on the contract in 2006 and 2007. We are all professionals and not necessarily motivated by tokens and awards, but it speaks volumes when you set out to create wins for your client and they recognize you with their highest honors. Incidentally, 2007 was the last time the Construction Manager of the Year award was given, so I feel very confident saying we still hold that title and have not been unseated by the competition.

We are still creating wins for contractors and the agency on their contracts and have won yet another $50 million contract and a major contractor training and curriculum development contract worth about $600,000 since then. We have negotiated our recent contracts with our partners from 30% subconsultant engagements to 50/50 joint venture partnerships and are very proud of the success we created for our partners along the way. We shifted the paradigm and created a new norm that gives us a huge advantage over others.

I believe my timing was impeccable and my skills appropriate but my blessing from God is what kept me sharp and focused on creating wins and made it possible for our firm to land a "big fish" client in our initial years. My background working for a city construction agency from 1997 to 2001 and as a consultant from 1990 to 1997 has served me well and given me an edge against the competition. I had often heard stories of professionals who had quit their job at a major company then turned their former employers into their first contract. I really never imagined that it could actually happen but it did. If you can maintain relationships, avoid burning bridges and build a great reputation for working hard, then your chances to land a major contract right out of the box are great.

So if you are working at a firm that you want to be your first contract when you decide to leave, learn all you can learn, be the best you can be, and believe that it can happen. Your experience will be welcomed, your insight will be valuable, and your perspective will be sharp and well-informed, putting you in a position to immediately land a "big fish" client.

CHAPTER 8 - BOLD MOVES TO MAKE NOW!

* Make your last employer your first contracted client by fully understanding their motivation and each compelling aspect of their business.

* Learn their system and be prepared to spot new opportunities for innovation, and fix any problem areas in their existing programs.

* Become certified as a minority-, woman-owned or locally based business to appear on your clients' radar, as most large firms need to track their diversity spending.

* Allow your proposals to focus on areas where your clients have been challenged in the past, and become the hero with your solutions.

* Coordinate the right team of professionals to quickly produce the right results once your team has been selected.

* Assemble the financing you'll need in order to accommodate your "big fish" clients that have complex procurement and payment processes.

* Be the point person for the contract—even if you are the president of the firm—to develop confidence and trust with your clients.

CHAPTER 9

COMMUNITY SERVICE FOR YOUR BUSINESS

Effecting Servant Entrepreneurship

One thing I know about business is if you can create wins for others, ultimately you win, too. This is our mantra! We take pride in establishing strategic, tactical, well-thought out, long-term, planned victories for our clients and community partners. Over the years, since our company was established in 2002, we have led the firm with what we can do for others. NobleStrategy is a for-profit firm concerned with the bottom line at the end of the day. However, we also realize that we can be concerned with other elements that perhaps don't always show up on our bottom line but do add value to our existence.

Can you imagine the impact you could have on your market, industry or community if other businesses could grow off of your efforts? How valuable could you be if you could raise the specter of an entire business community or specialized market through your work alone? What would you pay to be the go-to firm in your industry or region because you quickly became a "thought leader" in a particular space and could help others figure out their problems? Imagine how great it could be for your business if you could be a "virtual stimulus plan" for those around you, creating good fortune and business opportunities for others every time you were involved. You would be magnetic, and, eventually, you would be rich!

No doubt, the laws of attraction would be rewarding you many times over, and folks who could stand close to you might even see their fortunes change for the better just by being around you. You would be filling a need. Not just a self-serving need but one that is consistent with improving the condition of the entire community, and for that you can take credit. Well, we do take credit for our efforts as they show up on others' bottom lines. We call it servant entrepreneurship, where we are always ready and willing to be a resource to others first and then make sure our efforts eventually translate to success for our firm.

Unfortunately, the success doesn't always come in the tangible form of cash. Sometimes it comes as value as a market leader, which we can use. Sometimes it's deep market penetration in a coveted space, which we can use. Sometimes the success shows up in building the resources of another firm for growth, which we can always use. Sometimes it shows up in the confidence a firm has in our capabilities to create a win, which we can definitely use. Each time we make these deposits in the "bank of good will and service," they grow with interest and we always seem to get a very handsome return based on how we do business.

In fulfilling this concept we have been able to translate extreme value to other firms, community partners and professionals through a collaborative, social style of giving. No, we are not scooping out ice cream on Fridays to clients and calling it social entrepreneurship. And, no, we are not overtly crusading to "save the pandas" in all of our efforts—even though our efforts toward sustainability and green construction, which are part of our genetics, *will* actually preserve pandas who live off rapidly renewable materials like bamboo. What we are doing is making the most of our firm as a resource for those working in our industry and region. We have been operating with a servant entrepreneurship mentality and it has consumed our firm and our firm's offerings. The resulting servant/social platform takes shape in the context of our firm being a resource for others to grow and develop.

Building Others' Bottom Lines

When we looked at our year-end revenue for 2009 we were pleased to have earned approximately $3 million in fees. But we still felt that we had a long way to go. Remember, we set out to be a $100 million company and, although we were not performing any at-risk work where the costs of the actual project are included in the revenue totals, we still had a great year. After all, only 8% of U.S. small businesses earn more than a million dollars in revenue anyway. But while it was a major accomplishment to build approximately $3 million in consulting fees alone, we still had major work to do if we were going to reach the $100 million mark some day. Then we realized that some of the success other firms were having around us could be traced back to our mentoring services and lessons we taught.

Instead of questioning this natural progression, we decided to embrace it and started to promote the fact that we could add to your bottom line, no matter what stage your firm was in. We used slogans in our contractor training and mentoring programs, like "Tools to Grow Your Business at Any Level" since we felt we could positively impact most any business we worked with. Our mentoring and train-

> **MAKE A BOLD MOVE**
>
> *Build another firm's bottom line through extending what you've learned. Emerging firms can translate lessons learned from their own problem stages to other startups who haven't yet reached that point. Don't be afraid to teach someone else how to avoid the mistakes you made in order to improve their chances for success.*

ing efforts continued to grow as we earned more credibility with contractors who felt we were a helpful answer to their growth needs. We became a resource for contractors working on public projects throughout New York City and often had the opportunity to introduce them to larger prime contractors and construction agencies where they would immediately benefit from new opportunities.

This concept became contagious and started to spread like wildfire. We found ourselves handling more and more requests for mentoring and contractor outreach services. Although we always maintain that we want to establish a healthy book of business concentrated on construction management opportunities, we were not about to let the emerging contractor training and mentoring services, which we had grown accustomed to performing very well, fall off the table. The need to further develop this niche business has led us to create an offering we call the NobleStrategy Institute of Construction Management, where we provide customized training and contractor mentoring for emerging firms and Fortune 500 companies seeking to diversify their procurement spend.

We quickly charted our course and were able to successfully market how we could assist contractors' development and growth through our expertise and construction management perspective. You might be asking, *how much is this market worth and who is paying if the emerging contractors are not the ones funding their efforts to build capacity?* Since each major publicly funded project in most cities and states requires some form of minority, women-owned or local business participation, as well as workforce development for providing jobs to area residents, it can be a huge pool.

For projects valued at least $10 million, fee generation can be anywhere from 1% to 3% ($100K to $300K) for diversity-based consulting services, including workforce utilization planning, contractor outreach and capacity building and training. If the average assignment yields roughly $200K per year and you can win three of these types of assignments, as low hanging fruit not only will you be in a position to assist others' growth, you will be on your way to billing roughly $600K in fees in a single year. If this type of contractor assistance only accounted for nearly 20% of your business, you would already be doing $3 million in sales, which is tremendous in any market but especially in a recession! For some firms, generating $600K in fees alone would be significant. If you actually become good at what you do and others could see your value, and this type of work grew to be a larger portion of your projects (40%), or the size of the projects increased (over $100 million), you could swiftly confirm revenues of $1 million to $3 million per year, achieving your desired ***multimillion-dollar business success in less than 500 days!***

Utilizing Business Resources for a Cause

For entrepreneurs ready to make an impact, take a look at what a community can do for you and what you can do for the community. Most communities where business is located certainly have many offerings, such as local culture, cuisine, arts, entertainment, housing, social service organizations and professionals. But business owners can provide many offerings to their communities other than the services they provide for a fee. With a unique opportunity to impact the lives of residents and the local economy through the creation of jobs and other means of economic empowerment, business owners often find success in serving and supporting those they are supported by. Also, for most established business owners, there is a compelling desire to give back to the community once they feel that they have achieved their personal level of success. This is another natural progression or phenomenon that we should be co-opting instead of fighting against. The universe can use the energy from this path and create opportunities for successful business owners to "plug into the community machine" to make room for them and their generous contributions of time, talent and resources.

Surely, you remember a local pizzeria or hardware store in your town with pictures on the wall of the local Little League Baseball teams they supported. Yes, it does provide very basic advertising for the business owner but, more importantly, the business may be able to support and fund activities in the town that would otherwise not be available to the residents. This type of community involvement and awareness also allows for a closer connection between the community and the local entrepreneur. We explored how important relationships are in business in earlier chapters, and we know people do business with people they know and like. The community sponsorship could be one way to provide resources easily available to the business for the community's benefit.

Think about where and how you currently make your purchasing decisions in the community. Are they convenience-based or value-based? Do you shop at retailers closer to you or near other civic services so you can get a bunch of things done at once? Or are you willing to drive across town, sometimes out of your way, for the retail experience you get from another merchant? This is how people work—comfort, convenience, and familiarity. And once the connection is made it's usually relatively permanent.

In my town I can walk to a local food market, but most times I'll get in my car and drive 20 minutes away to go to a natural foods market for the value and experience they provide. Couldn't we change that entire paradigm through business-community connections? If you normally buy pizza from the national franchise near your home, would you be more likely to switch to the local independent pizzeria because they also sponsor town sports leagues or give donations to your school district on school promotional nights?

I definitely would go the extra mile to shop at a retailer that supplies my favorite charity with free turkeys every year for Thanksgiving. Remember, if all things are equal, then what will make the difference in how and where you buy? Usually, it's the intangibles, and I can tell you that a lot of retailers would score points with me for supporting causes that I feel strongly about. Not only is it good for me but it's good business for them. Most people would be willing to psychologically repay (in the form of support, top of mind consciousness, or purchasing loyalty) the institutions in their community for their commitment and continued support. In some cases it's no different for your emerging business. Whether you sell baked goods, repair cars, or perform interior decorating, landscaping, or architecture, your business can benefit from direct support from the people you serve.

Since most people would be persuaded by this, perhaps it's time for you to support more local causes. Not only is it good to give back but it will work for you and your business in ways you may not have thought of. After learning of your local sponsorship, you might be surprised to find that a high-profile potential client that you have been pursuing for months has children that play in a sports league that you have funded. All of a sudden you are getting face time through league games and local events that you pursued for such a long time. You might even get the meeting you've wanted because of this community connection. Perhaps the potential client would also learn about your civic commitment and, with all things being equal, possibly give your business a chance because of that community differentiator—your support of their favorite charity or cause.

Of course you never know this going into the deal, so you have to be doing it for the right reasons. But remember, the universe does have a strange way of evening out all rewards and consequences and you might just find a payday in your local community giving. The most positive thing that occurs, even if you can't realize this as an opportunity for your firm, is that you have provided a much needed resource in the community, allowing its vibrancy to remain intact. As long as the people are there, there is a chance they will support you. However, if you don't do your part to support the community and its programs and people leave, who will be there to support you in the long run? If you don't think it is your civic duty to support them, they will not be convinced that it is their duty to support you!

Championing a Local Cause

Think of the impact the Susan G. Komen foundation has had through local, national and international business organizations sharing in supporting awareness and research for breast cancer. It's pretty cool now but I never thought I would see the day when athletes in nationally televised sports programs—including some of the largest, swiftest, most gifted players on a football field—would don pink gloves and cleats, and use pink towels, with the NFL emblem on them all. My daughter really gets a kick out of reading the sports magazines with me as we look for all the close-up action shots featuring players in the pink apparel. Her favorite color is pink and she hasn't yet made the connection to why all these players are wearing so much girly pink in their uniforms.

The National Football League is a megamillion-dollar organization with multimillion-dollar broadcast and cable television deals that feature multiple high-profile Monday and Sunday night games where they can lend support for breast cancer awareness. They are using their largess and leverage to spread the word for the Susan G. Komen foundation and it bodes well for the NFL and its viewers. Not only are they raising consciousness, they're providing much needed funds for research to find a cure.

On October 4, 2010, ESPN's *Monday Night Football*—a 41-14 New England Patriots road victory over the Miami Dolphins—earned a 10.4 household coverage rating (9.0 U.S. rating), representing an average of 10,404,000 households, according to Nielsen. Each one of those households got the message loud and clear that the NFL is serious about breast cancer through the league-sponsored pink uniforms, cleats and towels. The NFL's reach here is huge and although this is a national example, this can be just as effective on a local level. So if the NFL's target market is largely male, what does this community or cause support have to do with the 13.9 million viewers that watched the Patriots–Dolphins game on October 4, 2010? Considering that there are women in the households and women watching TV, perhaps this expands their fringe market for the NFL, allowing them to invite more women into the game as fans. It may be that this connection can create a "top of mind consciousness" for women who have been touched by the moving support for breast cancer research shown by the NFL and now choose to buy and wear NFL apparel or don pink sports jerseys to show their own support.

As evidenced by the NFL example, businesses can gain a substantial benefit from championing local causes. Take a good look at the local causes or issues facing your community and see what you can do to help. As a business owner, your cumulative reach may be longer than that of any one individual because you communicate with such a large group of people on a regular basis. If your business is fairly successful there will always be people calling on you to provide services.

Wouldn't it be great if you could gain support for your local charity from the same folks you do business with, such as your accountant, insurance professionals, or health care providers? If your church is giving a free seminar on tax preparation, wouldn't it be great if the tax professional who counsels your business on a regular basis thought it important enough to you that she donate a couple of hours of her time on a Saturday morning to assist your congregation with tax preparation? Since you are in close proximity to business professionals who are your colleagues, couldn't you establish a roundtable or task force to tackle some major issues that haven't received the attention they require to be solved?

The "business of you" consists of your relationships, contacts, colleagues and resources that can be leveraged to solve many community issues. Volunteerism can be tiring but greatly rewarding and your personal efforts can and should be magnified through your business network and relationships. You can create the same power and leverage through your business networks as the NFL does using pink apparel in nationally televised football games.

One of the greatest joys I experience is serving as chairman for my fraternity's Black History Month program each year. The program is the Omega Psi Phi Fraternity, Inc. Eta Pi Chapter Black Wealth Initiative, which is focused on creating awareness around financial literacy, entrepreneurship and generational wealth accumulation in traditionally underserved communities. As a business owner and community leader, I feel especially grateful to spearhead this committee that works tirelessly to bring about change and improve the condition of the people in my community. I also enjoy the opportunity to work side by side with and gain support from professional friends whom I support during the year who are also willing to reciprocate for me. The support usually comes in the form of other business owners or service providers devoting their company and/or personal resources and time to assist in growing awareness for our causes. Similarly, I throw the total support of my firm into the tasks, calling on my professional friends to take part in the event.

MAKE A BOLD MOVE

Motivate your company or your entire industry to invest in a yearly community cause where you can get your business partners and associates to participate. Extend your reach and leverage your prominence to make a personal connection with nonprofits serving your community through board membership, committee leadership, or local service for a positive impact.

Something as seemingly simple as bringing well-dressed professionals to a Saturday morning school event to speak with students about entrepreneurship makes a huge impact in the lives of the kids who are ultimately shaping our communities each day. Providing positive role models for our youth through your business resources and relationships can complement efforts to stabilize communities once you become engaged.

If, tomorrow, you were selected Business Person of the Year by a local community organization, what would you do with it? Would you simply attend the event and take the trophy back to your mantle as a testament of how great you are? Would you tell others about the recognition so they could congratulate you on your success and perhaps envy your future actions? Or would you simply use the leverage and reach the platform creates to act on issues that may receive more attention and recognition now that you personify them as *Business Person of the Year*! Put your business to better use and be a resource to make things happen!

I have attended many fundraisers for colleagues and professional friends and gladly shared my time and lent my financial support to their causes. They may have been raising money for Haitian Relief after the devastating earthquake in January 2010 or creating awareness for the March of Dimes research on birth defects and infant mortality. Whatever the cause, I have seen firsthand how the weight of significant business leaders or an entire industry can lead efforts on awareness and charitable donations to support the community causes that people feel connected to.

Rutgers University has a great marketing campaign to create awareness around being the educational gem of the Garden State that asks you to *Think Globally, Act Locally!* It is powerful and you can do it. Make the right investments in your firm so you can utilize it to grow investments in the community at large for positive impact and change.

CHAPTER 9 - BOLD MOVES TO MAKE NOW!

* Adopt the mentality of serving others first, and watch your business grow.

* Get rich by distributing your time, talents and money freely to others less fortunate than you.

* Take on a community or neighborhood issue and create greater exposure for the cause by leveraging your business resources and industry position.

* Rally your colleagues and deliver impact by leading an industry task force, or start an association charged with fixing problems common to firms like yours.

* Grow your investment in the community by being a trusted and informative resource for elected officials, urban professionals and residents.

CHAPTER 10

BUSINESS POLITICS

Winning friends and influencing people has long been a popular topic in business. Of course, the reason you want to win friends and influence people is to gain access for the product, service, or experience you are working very hard to market. When dealing with your business associates, at some point, politics will inevitably come into play and you'd better know how to handle it. You wouldn't want to offend a potential client because of a personal view or action that could be perceived as a slight. Furthermore, you wouldn't want to work to establish your business through building relationships where no one was interested in having your trust or trusting you as a resource.

The title of this chapter is not meant to trip you up or suggest that you take the political aspect of your business lightly, it is meant to do just the opposite. This chapter will teach you the importance of understanding and intelligently playing in the business arena with respect to: building personal relationships, creating economic power through politics and strategy, and supporting legislators who might have a stake in your industry's success.

Personal Relationship Building

In the workplace, no one is a stranger to politics. Whether they are simple office politics or stepped up, high-stakes battles, you've no doubt been exposed to it and know that you can get burned if you don't play your cards right. In business it's no different.

Folks are prone to work with those they know and like, and sometimes folks they can benefit from or share a common cause with. It will be your duty to work to actively cultivate your "sweet spot" and form the right relationships with people, inside and outside of your business. In her book *Good is Not Enough* with Keith Wyche, Sonia Alleyne, an editorial director at Black Enterprise magazine, suggests that it is no longer acceptable only to be good at what you do and expect recognition and promotion in the workplace. If you've heard the expression "Going along to get along" then you are familiar with this concept.

Caucusing and building consensus around issues and thoughts is usually how things get done. You won't always have the option to steamroll your peers and slam through the office with only your thoughts and needs in mind. That strategy will definitely brand you an independent and perhaps a tyrant but will not contribute much to you successfully navigating office politics to get things done. Remember, all things being equal, people do business with people they know and like so yours is the never-ending task of displaying your magnetic personality to win friends and influence people—in the office, boardroom, or at the presentation table.

Whether you are the president of the company or a field associate, you must be well-liked internally and it never hurts when clients like you as well. If you are the president of the firm, you will need to attract and recruit top talent, and if they simply can't get along with you it will be difficult to build your firm. Did you ever wonder why there was a most popular award in high school? These folks were mastering their politics early on and learned the art and science of being well-liked. Of course, they didn't think they were preparing for life, work, or business, they just thought they were having fun. Nothing is different on this level, so play politics well, be well-liked, get along with others and have fun building your business and the relationships that come with it.

I love the game of golf, and golf can build lasting relationships in life and business. However, if you asked me 10 years ago if I would ever play golf, I probably would still be laughing today. I honestly felt there was no greater waste of time, land, money and valuable resources than the game of golf and its faithful participants. In 2001 when a pro golfer sued the PGA Tour in order to use a golf cart because of a birth defect in his leg, I can remember exclaiming, "This is ridiculous!" I couldn't understand what the big deal was and why some say he had an unfair advantage because he was granted the use of a cart during tournament play. Truth is I was ignorant about the stamina, rigor and skill required to play the game at the tournament level. Actually, I didn't understand at all the value of having use of a cart while everyone else had to walk.

When I started playing, I quickly became a sympathizer and learned that golfers are truly pro athletes. I also learned that some of the best relationships can be built playing a recreational game of golf. According to the PGA there are only about 28,000 professional golfers but approximately 50 million people play the sport. Although the professionals get paid to play, the general golf playing public stands to gain more from the game in terms of building quality relationships each and

> **MAKE A BOLD MOVE**
>
> *Use golf to build key relationships by finding key executives you know but perhaps have not been able to spend any meaningful time with and engage them in a discussion on playing golf. Immediately invite them out to play a round at a semi-private golf club. They will be impressed by the fact that you belong to a private club and usually will not miss the opportunity to play a round with someone they may like. Usually non-members can play at private clubs for a fee.*

every time a round is played. What better way to let your guard down and get to know someone—to see if you would like doing business with them—than a round of golf, which equates to a five-hour "trial run" out in the fresh air and beautiful landscape most courses provide.

The other good thing about the game is if you are trying to impress a senior-level executive or business colleague, and perhaps they don't play all that well, they will immediately be interested in your game, which will provide conversation points. Furthermore, when neither of you are much good at the game, it becomes a great equalizer, bringing the senior-level executive down a few pegs, so now you really have more in common and can talk on several levels. She can't hit the ball straight and neither can you! It may even provide some laughs throughout the day. But it will also create an opportunity for you to get to know one another in a very relaxed atmosphere. When the time has been spent and the relationship is on its way, then perhaps you'll want to discuss more opportunities for mutual business.

It's key to start out by listening and learning about your partner's business and perhaps how you could support what they do. Never, ever, get on the golf course and use the hard sell method to try to win business. It will definitely ruin your relationship and probably the rest of the afternoon since you two will be stuck with each other for the next several hours.

I was fortunate enough to meet a titan in business who ultimately became one of my mentors in 2009. While my firm had been selected by Black Enterprise as a Small Business of the Year finalist, this gentlemen's firm had been selected as the 2009 Black Enterprise Company of the Year, with sales of over $200 million. Even though we met at the magazine's annual Entrepreneurs Conference in Detroit, Michigan in May 2009, I didn't really get an opportunity to have a lasting conversation or build a relationship with the CEO early on. I did, however, learn that we were both members of Omega Psi Phi Fraternity, Inc., both having pledged the fraternity as undergraduate students.

When I pledged Omega Psi Phi Fraternity, Inc. and was initiated through the Gamma Epsilon chapter at Hampton University in the spring of 1987, I don't think I realized the breadth and wealth of personal and professional bonds that would be with me for life. Even though the CEO was managing a major organization with over 4,000 people and several business divisions, I had somewhat of an instant connection with him. We were both on the conference's program celebrating business achievement and, although I could have been considered the opening act as a Black Enterprise potential awardees, I was also a member of the same illustrious fraternity. We immediately shared a couple of things in common. We talked briefly and I congratulated him on his selection as Company of the Year.

MAKE A BOLD MOVE

Always ask a question—even when you know the answer. When you are in a crowded seminar and trying to establish your firm, make a bold move by asking your question but, of course, stating your name, your business, and how you create value first. People are usually shy and you can always score by getting the first question in and letting everyone know you are in the room. Make it a good, thought-provoking question or just use the question to take the conversation where you want it to go.

In early January of 2010, I attended the Rainbow PUSH Wall Street Initiative Conference for financial and economic equality, led by Jesse Jackson Sr. Incidentally; Jesse Jackson Sr. is also a member of the Omega Psi Phi Fraternity, Inc. In attending my first panel on Strategizing Megadeals, Acquisitions and Joint Ventures, I was surprised to learn that the 2009 Black Enterprise Company of the Year CEO was leading the session. After his presentation, I was prepared with my questions and leapt to the floor to raise my hand for recognition. The CEO quickly called on me and yielded the room to me. I stated my name, company and interest in the conference but also reminded him that we had met in Detroit the previous year when he received his award.

I asked a very perturbing question about emerging businesses controlling acquisitions and joint ventures over larger well-established firms. I was really looking for some executive education and real life answers to how smaller firms gain enough respect and credibility to control joint ventures with larger mainstream partners, which his firm had just completed by acquiring a much larger firm. His simple answer was, "That's a good question and a long story. We need to do lunch." Yes, I thought he was joking. But after his complete response I made my way to his seat and received his contact information along with his promise to call and set a date for lunch. He followed through and so did I. As a result, I received some executive education and lunch in Center City, Philadelphia several weeks later.

We had a lot to discuss and shared a lot in common based on our school backgrounds and fraternity experiences. The CEO had earned his undergraduate degree from North Carolina Central University, which is a historically black college and university. He and I played in the same sports conference, CIAA, years ago. Our lunch led to future appointments to play golf and we have shared several rounds, allowing me to build a relationship with and learn from a CEO of a $200 million firm. Our relationship still exists and I continue to support him in his professional endeavors and manage to play golf with him when his travel schedule allows. I have been a resource to him for information in the New York and Northern New Jersey market, and know that our relationship will be even more fruitful in the future.

Creating Economic Power Through Politics and Strategy

While businesses survive and thrive off of cash, there are other currencies that can be critical to your business success, such as power, influence and control. Even though you desire to build your business into a financial power, would you be willing to settle for being the voice of a few hundred local businesses that could shape, support or control a community issue or even an election? I certainly would.

One of the critically important missing pieces in most entrepreneurs' plans to establish their firms is political strategy, which can and should be coordinated for economic empowerment. This includes how your firm is perceived on particular business issues and perhaps what message you are sending. Sometimes supporting a cause can show where you stand on a particular topic, but standing silent on a cause or issue can illustrate how you feel about a situation as well. This has less to do with political affiliation and simply making donations to candidates than what you might have perceived as the point of intersection between business and politics. This concept has much more to do with leveraging your position in the community for the greater good.

If you employ people or produce a product, service, or experience that is utilized by those in your area, then you can quickly exchange your political capital for influence and access to those who govern the community your business is in. Either way, you will quickly find that, depending on the success of your business, people will be interested in what you have to say—in your industry, market, or community. Make sure that when you decide to speak on issues, your communication gets you what you want and you actually reach the folks you want to influence.

Have a Political Plan

So how much money and time have you allocated to your local legislators in the hopes of executing your political strategy for economic empowerment and influence? You become an instant asset to those in local government who are in position to make a difference. These are often the same folks who rely on staying in office to execute their plans for the community and need your time, influence, resources and money. Be sure, as you develop a strategy to support local initiatives that you understand what the end game is for you and your business. Are you expecting to lead a community initiative or chair a community group that will hold legislative power with elected officials? Can your group get things done, like changing laws and improving conditions for those who may be

> **MAKE A BOLD MOVE**
>
> *Use your resources—such as money, market position, influence, or even a planned event—to raise awareness for issues that you might be able to provide some proactive solutions for, through organizing a local task force. Mobilize your group and bring your concerns and potential solutions to the local elected officials, and be a resource to effect change.*

employed by your business? Can those initiatives support the further growth and development of your business through tax credits, incentives, and zoning requirements? Now is the time to figure it all out since this will be a critical element of your political plan.

Most people are very familiar with supporting local politicians through donations and mobilizing voting efforts, but the key is being able to lobby and leverage those same officials in the direction of your causes, community concerns, or business issues. Once you become a trusted resource and, in some cases, donor, you will no doubt gain access to bring issues and concerns to the table. Your voice is even more powerful when you are representing a group of local businesses sharing the same concerns. Whether you c*hair a local task force tackling a major issue or create a business association representing folks in your industry, take advantage of the inherent leadership and influence your business can give you and work your plan for economic empowerment through political strategy.*

Supporting Local Legislators

Entrepreneurs often get opportunities to meet and greet elected officials, agency directors and local legislators based on their business, industry and position in the marketplace. The elected officials, agency directors and local legislators depend on the businesses in the community to either be advocates for their plans or to advise them on what issues matter most to folks working to create wealth and economic power. Politicians often also need local businesses to fund initiatives and spread the word on progress. If you are in a position to create and grow jobs in a community as a business owner, then whether you realize it or not, you have political influence and can create economic empowerment.

State, city and local leaders are often assigned to chair or serve on specific committees that might be directly related to your business or industry. Develop your access and lobbying efforts to make sure they know you are a trusted resource that can communicate concerns and solutions on those topics. Elected officials often lament about people only coming to them when they need a job or have a friend or family member that needs help out of a sticky situation, but there is tremendous opportunity to change that dynamic and become a resource for local leaders, helping them during difficult times.

If you can use this natural flow of opportunities to your advantage, you can quickly gain market position and become influential in your industry through political strategy. Suppose a state senator was charged with developing a plan to provide greater access to loans and business opportunities for local minority- and women-owned businesses and needed help. If this is an area you have been focused on, perhaps you have figured out what the problem is and have some new and creative means of solving the issues. Be a resource and go to the senator with a well-developed plan that they can integrate into their way of thinking. If you are successful at presenting new ideas that have been vetted by the community and can gain support, your state senator will have developed a trusted resource that they can rely on to provide information and access for your industry.

Of course, your access may have to be gained through warm introductions and even some donations, but your value will be recognized and you will be on your way to playing in market that you were previously trying to figure out how to enter.

A Harlem Strategy

In contemplating our move to Harlem, New York, in early 2008, I realized that we would have to do some real relationship building in order to gain access and be accepted into the fabric of the community. We wanted to make a grand entry but also had a great deal of respect for the local business leaders and professionals who were already there and had been toiling away, working to build access and greater opportunities for local firms. We developed a strategy based on being a resource for the community, elected officials and local leaders. After all, our mantra is to be a "professional construction resource." So if we can cause you to win, ultimately we win as well.

Before we even thought about selling our services, we knew that if we could not be a resource to the community our mission might fail. We wanted to gain access to political leaders and were fortunate enough to have built some solid relationships that assisted us. We found extreme value in the business associations and chambers of commerce that existed in the community and supported them regularly. We met and quickly integrated into their world and became a resource for their alliances and their membership. In order to ensure that we would be welcomed and quickly established as a trusted resource, we decided to market our move to the community as part of our business strategy, which included a response to the recession and downturn in the economy that gripped the nation around 2008.

Our grand opening on July 9, 2009 was a great event attended by high-ranking city administrators, state and city elected officials, local community leaders, and current and potential clients. We planned an elaborate event with participation from local nonprofits, schools, media, restaurants and churches. Incidentally, creating even more exposure and hype, the popular NBC-TV drama *Law and Order* was filming on our block, directly in front of our office after the ribbon cutting celebration.

We took advantage of the fact that we were all going through the most severe recession our country had seen since 1931. Businesses were closing their doors and people were losing their jobs. The real estate crash had hit Harlem hard and while there was a flurry of new construction, condos remained empty, waiting for buyers. These were all issues that could be attached to a local "feel good" story. Local officials who were able to convince businesses to open new locations in their community could benefit as well. When a business comes to town, it brings its tax dollars, jobs and resources for spreading wealth in the community, and this was a real opportunity to tell a story we did not want to miss. We also noted that one of our public clients was spending almost $2 billion in the upper Manhattan community, including Harlem, which was another story that needed to be exposed. We grabbed both of these concepts and planned a way for local officials and agency directors to share in the success of our grand opening for a community benefit. After all, businesses overall were not opening in record numbers during the recession and they certainly had other options and incentives to locate in communities other than Harlem. It was our choice, our desire, and our story to contribute to the renaissance of a culturally rich and energetic community on the rise.

It was a very well-attended event and everybody won! We leveraged our decision to move in for the benefit of the community and immediately shared our resources and success with those who would ultimately elevate our firm's market position. The elected officials spoke, the bands played and the vibe was created for celebrating not just NobleStrategy's grand opening and move to the area but the confirmation and hope that the recession had not eliminated the opportunity to bring entrepreneurship and the pursuit of the American dream back into focus.

We had a great grand opening. We were introduced to the community and widely accepted with the support of key local leaders, agency directors and elected officials. We sent a clear message to the community, our clients, and competitors about who we are, who thought we were important enough to be with that day, and why they should know about our firm—all by utilizing a planned event that would have happened anyway. Because we understood the value in having a political strategy and being a resource for local leaders, we were able to score many benefits from what appeared to be a simple, one-time business grand opening announcing our entrance.

CHAPTER 10 - BOLD MOVES TO MAKE NOW!

* Work hard to build, maintain and master local political and relationship issues in order to thrive in your business.

* Remember that people do business with people they know and like, so get to know as many people as you can and be prepared to deliver value to each of the relationships you build.

* Develop your golf game and use it as an equalizer to open new relationships with folks you seek to do business with or those who can be a resource for your firm.

* Create and coordinate a group of local business owners seeking to increase their government relations and legislative support.

* Support local elected officials and inform them of critical issues facing your business, then help them solve the problems.

* Combat the effects of a slow economy and create a wave for your supporters to ride by launching your venture or new programs in less than favorable times.

CHAPTER 11

GETTING THE WORD OUT

Using a Social Strategy
(Marketing, Advertising and Promotions Plan)

How do you intend to spread the word about your new business or service? Do you have a huge marketing budget or access to an editorial news staff to promote your firm? I recommend that you first take stock of what you have, then assess how and when you can reach your intended market. Your available reach and time to market will ultimately depend on your cash flow, ability to build and sustain a campaign, and your access to other necessary resources.

In order to be successful you will have to plan a strategy to effectively promote your business based on creative methods and non-traditional marketing techniques. The traditional means may not even fit with your business but should still be evaluated for proper decision making. This can give you the leverage needed to quickly ramp up and be ready for the competition. By accessing the people you know and the people they know, you have the ability to use technology to quickly connect people in a marketing, advertising and promotions network.

This strategy can be aided by traditional and nontraditional techniques but, overall, will include people as the focal point of your efforts in lieu of money. Shaping the minds and perspectives of the people you get in front of will cause you to grow as a leader and allow messages to be spread virally by folks who get your message.

Market Yourself as a Thought Leader

MAP (Market-Advertise-Promote) - Business owners have the immediate opportunity to tackle issues facing their organizations and communities through leadership. Become an expert "thought leader" on special topics and you will be sought after as a speaker, decision maker and influential business leader. This becomes an instant means of promotion for your original and problem solving ideas and it also creates a perfect backdrop for clients wanting to learn more about your business.

Perhaps you edit a column or write a story on a particularly sensitive topic that leads to another story being picked up by a larger media outlet. Folks who have not heard of your business but compete in the same industry may be more inclined to listen longer when you, as "the expert," finally get a chance to speak. Perhaps they are being affected by the issue that you wrote about or have strong feelings about the cause that can create an initial conversation. In business, all types of ice breakers are useful for getting to the people you want to be with. If you can break the ice over a quick conversation about your last editorial piece, which appeared in the local paper, imagine the comfort level the reader or potential client might feel because they agree with your perspective.

Being a sought after thought leader has many more advantages than just being able to break the ice. Consider the opportunity to become an adjunct professor at a well-respected institution of higher learning. Surely, this would be a major shot in the arm for your expert status as well as your business credibility. Aligning your pursuits with those of a top-notch university that has recognized your achievement in business or work as an expert in your field can be immeasurable in providing the type of business promotions you couldn't buy, even if you tried.

If you are the visionary piloting the firm to success and happen to be engaged in shaping the minds of future leaders through research and curriculum delivery, imagine the symbolism now associated with your name, work and ideas. As you market your position as a respected adjunct professor, you can also indirectly build awareness and create exposure for the firm you created and are leading.

This concept quickly extends to specific situations and provides even more credibility based on timing and what is occurring in the environment. If you take a close look at the recession of 2008 (which actually began somewhere around October 2006), you would see that a vast majority of firms struggled and many even closed their doors. People lost jobs, business leads dried up, executives changed jobs and opportunities to grow emerging firms were almost nonexistent. But think of the credibility you could gain if you were a business leader or thought leader that piloted their operation through the recession with success. If your firm actually started to experience growth and you were hiring and actually making money in spite of all the turmoil around you, it would be very easy to sell your lessons learned—and your experiences.

The work of some tenured university professors is largely research-based and not always based on real world applications or experiences. You immediately gain an edge if your perspective is sharp and honed by business experiences matched with the academic rigor of an advanced degree and teaching expertise. Based on your knowledge, you will have created a position of power and influence from your combined business experience, status as an adjunct professor and expert thought leadership in your industry.

Make it happen, market it well and promote yourself and your business through expert status as a thought leader on specific issues.

Ability to Promote Industry Leader Status

Another quick means of getting the word out about your business is promoting your industry leader status. Of course, in order to do this you must stay in front of your industry and be on the cutting edge of research-based knowledge. You literally need to be *in front of your industry*, I mean actually standing in front of them, delivering information in the form of conference speeches or serving as an influential panelist on local seminar sessions.

Whether you typically attend national conferences for the information or the networking, you can be sure that influential leaders are drawn to these events. A great deal of press is generated from conferences since they serve as a snapshot of evolving industries and professionals at work. Cutting edge research is delivered, new techniques are examined and relevant

> **MAKE A BOLD MOVE**
>
> *Speak at national conferences and industry events as a leader or problem solver who has developed cutting edge research or a strong professional opinion based on experience. Follow industry trends and seize the opportunity to deliver timely information to those who have not yet figured out a solution for the pressing issues facing the market.*

knowledge, opinions and information are always on display. If you can create enough data to suggest that you are relevant in the industry, the only thing left to do is navigate your way to the podium for speaking opportunities. These opportunities allow you to not only deliver your perspective and knowledge on a particular subject but they also allow your industry peers and other professionals to recognize you for your ideas and perspectives. Joining industry associations and attending conferences can also provide access to grow and promote your business in ways you may not have considered.

Call for Speakers and Decision Makers

So where are the most prolific conferences held in your area? Where are the opportunities to cross over into another industry that directly correlates with your business or solutions? How could you leverage your expert status to affordably expand your reach? Do you have to travel to Florida or Las Vegas, or do you already reside in the metropolitan area and can easily access conventions in New York City? Start identifying the top 10 industry conferences that come to your area where you feel you could market yourself as an expert. In most big cities, established convention centers publish a calendar of annual conventions and conferences. Furthermore, if you target a couple of industries where your information would be valuable, you can quickly find the conferences that professionals attend regularly. A thorough scan of their website will lead you to critical information and criteria they use in requesting proposals for speakers. Get familiar with the term "Call for speakers," which is the industry's request to evaluate what value you might be able to bring to their members and conference attendees.

Strategically attend conferences to become familiar with the folks who make the decisions in the organization about conference speakers. It always helps to create a relationship with the industry or organization that you will target. Remember—people do business with people they know and like. You will need to keep this in mind when applying the strategies for success mentioned in earlier chapters.

The first couple of times you attend an annual conference, use your time wisely to get to know the event staff and the folks who coordinate the agendas. If the conference is organized by a magazine, do your best to meet the folks who create and craft the magazine on a regular basis. Be prepared to offer something to them before you ask what you can get; be a resource for them and things will work for you. You will have a great advantage if you are well-established in your industry as a thought leader by this time. And if you have credentials and a new perspective on what is happening in the industry, you are a definite candidate for offering your knowledge at the event.

Associations often represent political movements and professional constituencies that get their issues heard but, more importantly, they get access to those who can improve their business conditions. Partnering programs exist and matchmaking becomes paramount in connecting business industry leaders for familiarity and deal flow. Once you master this effort, you will find that you are able to highlight your experience and become very well known without using marketing dollars and just by leveraging all available business resources instead, including your industry status.

Leverage Social Networks, Not Money for Advertising and Promotions

Since you have already assessed your shoestring marketing budget and come to the conclusion that you must rely on creativity and not dollars, be ready to leverage all aspects of your network. Some sales professionals get jobs based solely on how many people they know. So how many people do you know? If you could deputize your friends, family, and business colleagues to spread the word about your business, could it expand your reach? You would absolutely extend far past what your initial marketing dollars could do if you harnessed the power of technology and social media.

By now, I'm sure you have heard stories of folks gaining popularity through social media strategies and networks. But most people in business still haven't figured out how social media strategies can build your business. If you are considering developing a strategy that includes sending daily tweets on Twitter or posting daily updates on Facebook about what you ate for breakfast, you have it all wrong. At some point, you can and will develop a following based on your leadership status and people will be interested in your every move. But it won't happen right out of the box. Social media strategies have to be carefully planned and given the appropriate time to develop. Remember— we are talking about using social media strategies for marketing advertising and promoting opportunities, but not for selling.

The first mistake you could make is trying to use your social media strategy to sell over the Internet. People quickly figure that out and will not follow you (or spread your gospel) once they realize that's all you're about. Your strategy should be informative for the followers you hope to gain and give them some reason to spend their free time with you. Americans are spending more time on the Internet and using mobile devices to access information as a daily way of life. According to comScore reporting, the number of people using their mobile devices on a daily basis to access news and other information more than doubled between January 2008 and January 2009, reaching 22.4 million. Since more and more people are turning to their devices, it makes sense to develop strategies that provide interplay between the way people conduct their lives.

Once someone finds an interesting article or perspective on a topic online, it becomes very easy to manage, share and spread that information across multiple networks. If you are the expert and it is your information that family, friends and business colleagues are exporting to their networks, imagine the reach you gain. You are instantly communicating with people you don't know, people who are developing an affinity for you. If you are able to build a following that becomes a community of trust whereby people know you are providing current and credible information, your strategy can quickly take shape and create competitive advantage and exposure for your firm.

In the summer of 2007, I started teaching as an adjunct professor at New York University in the construction management degree program offered through the Schack Institute of Real Estate. The class was Managing On-Site Operations in a Construction Firm. That topic was second nature to me and I delivered it very comfortably, using my work experience, technical resources and textbook materials. But as we studied best practices of some of the largest and oldest construction management firms, I noticed a very disturbing and pronounced void. It was evident that these firms with hundred-year-old histories could not quickly pivot and adapt to developing social trends.

If ever there were a downside to operating a multi-generational organization, it would be in periods where the technology advanced so quickly that it outpaced the generations' implementation. Simply put, if you cannot understand where technology has gone, you will not be able to use it to your advantage. But others who understand will.

MAKE A BOLD MOVE

Use social media strategies, including Facebook, Twitter, and LinkedIn, to provide industry knowledge as a resource instead of trying to sell over the Internet. Focus on building a community of trust where people value your opinions as credible and perhaps they will want to follow you for what you can do for them. Then, and only then, can you figure out what you want to sell them.

So as we researched some of the biggest and brightest stars in the New York construction market, I noticed that the CEOs of these companies didn't use much social media strategy. I often remarked that it was hard to believe that CEOs who were influential in business had no desire or understanding of how to spread viral marketing information to extend their brand to new generations of followers for increased market position.

As the recession started to grip the business community, it became necessary to use whatever methods you could to gain competitive advantage. Social media became one of the main strategies and opportunities utilized to slow the effects of a more competitive market consuming you. So I thought, *if the CEO of a 100-year-old firm doesn't use Twitter to keep his industry and followers abreast of what is developing in his market, then perhaps it is an opportunity for a firm like ours to utilize the tools that others didn't quite understand.* I thought, *the folks who I want to hire are the folks who understand new technology.* I also knew that my business could quickly advance our market position by using the tools created to eliminate the size advantages many companies held over their competitors.

At the time, Twitter was in the early stages. Social media networks such as Twitter, Facebook and LinkedIn are now

113

staples in most professionals' bag of tricks and have become outlets people use for information, knowledge and industry trends. According to a report from Forrester Research, 55.6 million U.S. adults—just shy of one-third of the population of adult internet users—visited social networks at least monthly in 2009, an increase from 18% in 2008.

The exploding potential in using this type of strategy will allow your emerging firm to leapfrog the competition and establish more followers than the competition has clients. Eventually, that edge can translate into market influence and business opportunities if managed correctly. With over 500 million people using Facebook worldwide, imagine if you could command one-tenth of a percent of the total to promote your good business news and information. That would translate into approximately 500,000 people singing your praises. Most start-ups would never have the budget to reach that number of people, but with a solid social media strategy, it could happen for you. Take the 300 million users of Twitter and the 100 million-plus users of LinkedIn and the market potential to leverage these networks becomes staggering.

Our firm utilized Twitter, Facebook and LinkedIn very successfully as part of our social media strategy. By posting updates two to three times a week and adding followers each day, our firm maintains a connection with our general public that creates an instant feedback loop. We can quickly gauge what folks are thinking about our ideas and how they value our information, comments and research. We have even successfully utilized these services to recruit star employees in a fraction of the time and cost it took several years ago.

Our firm has been able to quickly gauge the benefit here and turned to developing a social media strategy, including creating a Facebook company page, Twitter account and a LinkedIn profile. Over time we learned to use other network services such as Delicious, HootSuite, PingFm, TweetDeck, Tumblr, and TubeMogul as part of our strategy. Not only did we create momentum and a following for the information I personally sent out but we also took advantage of increased video capabilities and started distributing high-definition content across the Internet.

After completing production on a slick promotional video for American Express Open Forum, we created a YouTube channel to spread the news. The American Express video was great even though it only played on the Open Forum website for business owners, but technology allowed us to export that content to anyone who had access to YouTube and it launched our viral marketing efforts. There are at least 40 social networks that can assist you in building your social media strategy, and all are well worth researching to fit your needs.

Our social media effort started merely as an opportunity to develop a community of trust around emerging business issues, specifically contractor training and development in the minority- and women-owned business sectors. It has become a business model and marketing plan strategy to build consensus as a market leader and industry expert on many issues business owners face. Having dealt with many challenging start-up issues and categorizing many creative means to clear those obstacles, I have developed a credible and informed perspective that is used in our company efforts for branding, promoting, creating awareness and gaining exposure.

CHAPTER 11 - BOLD MOVES TO MAKE NOW!

* Market your services by deputizing friends, family and satisfied clients to spread your gospel and create impactful word-of-mouth advertising.

* Promote yourself as a thought leader or industry expert to highlight your expertise and your firm's capabilities.

* Obtain industry leader status through speaking engagements, conferences and panel discussions to further commercialize your knowledge and business success.

* Use the viral value of social media networks to build a community of trust first, without trying to sell over the Internet.

* Publish and distribute your best promotional content across multiple platforms on the Internet for immediate and extensive exposure.

CHAPTER 12

GO GREEN FOR MORE MONEY AND MORE MARKETSHARE

**Score big and lead your industry with
sustainability, environmental consciousness
and social responsibility.**

By now, I know that you want to be successful at what you are doing. I also know you are willing to make the commitment and cultivate the passion necessary to see it through. But don't miss the opportunity to harness the current world focus on our changing environment for your benefit. What have you wondered about this new green revolution? Have you figured out how to make money out of the notion of sustainability and social responsiveness? Are you ready to add a new dimension to your firm? Hopefully, you know enough about our world economy to see the value and importance of conserving our natural resources and creating alternative energy resources. But do you know how it is all connected to your business?

With the uprising in many oil-producing and -exporting countries and the cost of oil hovering around $150 per barrel (as of April 2011), we can no longer rely on our traditional supply of fossil fuels. However, we can now embrace increased awareness about the environment as a planned "green strategy" to sustain ourselves and generate revenues at the same time. Furthermore, now is the time to increase your market share by leading your firm and industry with new offerings. Developing an approach that embraces sustainability and environmental consciousness is extremely relevant today and a very good complement to your current business model. Your firm wins by creating a marketable strategy that includes your professional skills, business processes and the manner in which you deliver your product, service or experience. Consider developing your green strategy as a means to differentiate and expand your professional skills. If you can acquire the expertise and, in some cases, the certification that would allow you to be considered an authority on the practice of sustainability, you could gain leverage and opportunity for your business.

In 2003 I was focused on managing the design and construction of 20 to 25 large public schools in New Jersey. I was required to evaluate design professionals and critique their proposals and technologies used in the planning process for the new schools. It required a lot of work and research but I knew I could only be successful if I could raise my level of expertise to match the "experts" that were presenting the emerging technologies and alternative energy designed systems. Not wanting to be out of the loop in the architectural and engineering discussion for the new buildings, I began to research the requirements for professional sustainability accreditation by the United States Green Building Council. The USGBC had developed a rating system and criteria for building professionals to be measured by in order to achieve or signify their commitment to the principles of sustainability.

MAKE A BOLD MOVE

Take the time to research, cross train and become certified in emerging technologies that will create differentiation. This can potentially render the competition non- existent, thus creating an uncontested marketplace for you.

Over the course of the next 12 months, I added to my body of knowledge by researching the various codes and regulations that made up the Leadership in Energy and Environmental Design (LEED) rating system. After a full year of study and practical application at work, I took the required exam in January 2004, passed on my first attempt and became a LEED accredited professional, which I started to market. Even though I was not running my own business at the time, it was critically important for the director of design and construction of such a large school district to have the qualifications and capabilities to lead by example and set the stage for the sustainability revolution as it was ushered in at my place of business.

Today I continue to maintain my LEED credentials, taking all the required professional development hours needed and documenting to USGBC so I can actively utilize the USGBC sustainability logo and the LEED accredited professional designation, LEED AP, after my name. This is a valuable differentiator that suggests I am a practitioner of sustainability and regulated by a governing body of industry professionals. Each time I use the LEED AP designation, my credibility is instantly proven as a practicing authority on the subject that can and should be marketed as part of your green strategy.

In just three short years after that, having participated in the design and construction process on two $60 million high schools and four $30 million elementary schools, I was well prepared and able to market myself as a practicing sustainability professional. Once I left my job at the school district and started my venture, I immediately started to market sustainable design and construction practices as part of the services my firm offered. It quickly became a differentiator for our construction management firm, since most of the people who had that expertise at the time were either architects or engineers. Our green strategy became a part of our brand and constituted a huge competitive advantage within the traditional construction management industry. At that time (2006) there were very few minority-owned businesses participating in the sustainability discussion at all. Although, today, it might be commonplace for some larger concerns, smaller, more diverse firms still face this barrier for business, similar to the digital divide we've worked so hard to overcome.

Being one of a few firms that understood the value of sustainability on a project and its benefit to owners, we have been able to promote a new industry offering consisting of our sustainable construction management solutions, which we termed LEED CM™. LEED CM™ is the practice that involves an accredited professional with a construction management perspective and expertise to manage the elements of the LEED building rating system, as well as the education of contractors, subcontractors and vendors in obtaining and managing the required documentation in the field during the construction of a project. We quickly realized that if the process only required architects and engineers to design a perfectly sustainable system, who would be responsible for making sure it was built according to plan? This is typically the job of the construction manager. Similarly, your project won't get built by using a great architect or engineer but by engaging a competent and experienced construction manager to synthesize the process and coordinate the building efforts according to your plan. LEED CM™ strives to provide owners the same assurance and value as it relates to the technical aspects of sustainability and energy efficiency while reducing the traditionally negative impacts of the construction process.

We found our niche and, in 2007, started performing these very same services for one of the largest and oldest construction management firms in New York City as part of the major rebuilding effort in lower Manhattan after the terrorist attacks of September 11, 2001. The $1.8 billion project consisting of 104 floors located at Ground Zero in lower Manhattan will include substantial sustainability elements for the tenants and all building occupants. We have successfully contributed to the sustainable aspects of this project since 2007 and look forward to its completion as a testament to the will and resilience of New York City and our great nation. We are very proud to be connected to this project and thrilled that our green strategy was harnessed for one of the largest and most recognizable projects in the world.

Just like the Industrial Revolution of the 1940s or the technology revolution of the 1980s, we are facing an energy and sustainability revolution that has been occurring since the early 2000s that is changing our lives and the way we do business. Each day, more and more organizations and individuals are trying to find better ways to cope with the pressing need to mitigate the effects of global warming and other environmental challenges. Furthermore, this discussion, which includes environmental considerations, conservation of natural resources and energy efficiency through the use of emerging technologies, constitutes the "green revolution," which proves to be a great opportunity for those who understand it.

The possibilities to solve complex or ordinary problems simply by utilizing concepts that benefit the environment and make a strong statement about who you are and what social benefit you will make seem endless. International markets are sprouting and cottage industries are being created, which is raising the awareness of the general public about these sensitive issues. Each day, new businesses are being formulated and existing businesses are being sustained by effectively going green as a practical solution and form of corporate consciousness, market position and branding. And you should not be left behind. By viewing the achievement gap in most public schools across the nation, you can starkly feel the effects of the digital divide and how missing out on the technology revolution can stack the deck against you.

This digital divide, which is considered the lack of access to emerging technologies, applications and their resources, has caused a severe drop off in learning for poor, undeserved and minority communities. If emerging businesses don't manage the green revolution and access to sustainable technologies, they run the risk of creating a new divide that will make it even more difficult for those businesses to compete in difficult markets.

Sustainability is defined as being capable of being continued at a certain level without harm or impact to the built environment. Imagine your company and what it takes to keep it going, and even think about what will be required to make it grow. Think deeply about the effects of your business and what it produces as by products. Does your operation pollute air in communities? Does your product ship in packaging that takes years and years to break down in a landfill? Does your service require you to waste natural resources or consume large amounts of raw non-renewable materials? Does the new building you're constructing have a huge material import cost that will ultimately contribute to your carbon footprint during and after the construction? (Cumulative greenhouse gas emissions produced by you and your burning fossil fuels to create building materials also creates carbon dioxide in the earth's atmosphere.)

Understanding how sustainability matters and how the environment's well being can play a role in the development of a successful green strategy should be critical to any 21st century business operation. Furthermore, environmental consciousness and sustainability are not only meant to be external strategies but rather tools to be employed within any organization to reduce its consumption of energy and natural resources and lessen overall operation costs, ultimately making the business more competitive. Get this one right and you can sustain yourself whether you are marketing green products or simply running a very well-oiled "green machine" that pays less for its utilities, preserves natural resources and operates at optimal conditions year round.

Are there firms that are known merely for their attempts to go green in a particular market where there was no emphasis previously? Can you identify markets that have been created by leveraging the public sentiment for environmental consciousness? Is this a viable strategy for you no matter what you are selling? These are all very good questions, but even better answers will be provided in your understanding of how to effectively "go green" in your business as soon as you can.

Internal Benefits of Going Green

So if you haven't yet grasped how going green within your internal operation can be beneficial, consider the following advantages of adopting a green strategy. In striving to be more competitive and grow your business, you have to either sell more stuff, pay less for the stuff you sell, or reduce your operating expenses and fixed costs. Focusing on reducing your fixed costs will produce savings and allow you to implement your green strategy with an overall energy audit at your place of business. In addition to gaining greater efficiency on energy and operating equipment, an energy audit and assessment can yield valuable benefits in occupant comfort, usage and modified consumption behaviors and awareness for your office or facility.

Review your operations procedures and length of operation each day of the week, then consult your energy bill. Do you think you could benefit if you reduced your energy consumption by 20%? It may not sound like much, but the 20% you save, year after year, not only makes you environmentally conscious but adds cash to your balance sheet. Not many people are willing to include the benefit of preserving natural resources and using less energy on a financial statement but, trust me, the computation is already there, you just need to recognize it. Even if you slashed your electric bill by focusing on lighting alone— which would not be difficult—you stand to gain major savings for years to come. Through technology and the evaluation of how your business operates, you can employ the right cost savings measure, whether it is more efficient lighting or reducing work hours, to match productivity and peak times.

While I always wanted to try reducing our firm's energy consumption through reducing work hours, I initially thought I would lose productivity and wasn't able to come up with the right plan until recently. The initiative for energy reduction would become part of a total sustainability plan that would produce many benefits, including but not limited to, increased employee morale and cash flow management. In the summer of 2010, as our firm coped with the ever present effects of the recession, I devised our sustainability plan to allow us to weather the storm of the bad economy and provide some much needed benefits based on the sacrifices we were asking people to make.

Due to a financial squeeze on city contracts and budget woes, one of our largest clients asked us to reduce staff by 30% at the end of 2009. This carried into the first quarter of 2010 and by April we were faced with at least four rounds of salary reduction. In Phase I we eliminated positions and released people. In Phase II we moved some people from full-time to part-time employment. In Phase III we reduced some salaries by 5% or 10%. By Phase IV we had further reduced salaries for our executive staff and created our Summer Sustainability Initiative. We examined our energy consumption and hours of operation and decided to close our offices early on Fridays during the summer months.

After careful review, we noticed that productivity was often low on Friday afternoons after lunch and we did not receive many inbound calls. We also knew that if employees could plan on being away from the office or out of the office early on Fridays—contingent on a modified work schedule during the week—it could improve employee morale. Closing the offices early on Friday contributed to reducing our energy consumption by reducing lighting and operational energy usage (copy machines, microwave ovens, refrigerators, cell phone chargers, etc.). We did, however, ask employees to work harder during the first four days of the week so that we would not miss much in productivity by shelving Friday afternoon.

If Friday represented 20% of the work week, we had to consider what being away from the office (and still communicating effectively) for that day would save us during the months of July and August. It wasn't exactly a 20% savings but it did promote a consciousness to employees that we wanted to be sustainable by all means. I had always wanted a reduced summer work schedule and this was our way of achieving it. We still did the work by utilizing technology to forward calls and rotate independent coverage in the office, but we also made a substantial impact on our employees through an internal environmental consciousness and green strategy!

External Benefits of Going Green

We made the conscious decision to market our sustainability and green strategy as our differentiation and, in some cases, our competitive advantage over other firms. The same way we could benefit through an internal green strategy, we saw the opportunity to benefit from an external one. Promoting your social responsibility and environmental friendliness in your business operations is something that should not be ignored. I'm not simply talking about marketing green strategies as a trend but rather using solid business practices that produce a positive effect on the public and the environment each and every day. Could you gain a competitive advantage over other firms because of your environmental stance? Could you win new clients on the basis of what your firm's social consciousness is? Might you be able to sustain customers in a new market because your approach is recognized as "planet-" or "earth-friendly?" I say yes to all of the above and so should you for increased opportunities and potential profits.

In the real estate market, developers are often cited for not being invested in certain projects. Sure, they invest a lot of money but usually the plan is to market, build and get out by either turning the property over to a management company or selling to other investors, or even individual owners. You would think that developers wouldn't have much interest in implementing external green strategies if they weren't holding their properties for long periods of time. The whole notion of the value of sustainable projects is that, over time, the calculated benefits will exceed the first cost required for implementation.

The first cost is the investment you must make up front to harness the technology or implement a new green strategy. If your payback period is four to six years, usually it makes sense for you to amortize your first cost over that period of time. If you are a long-term player, you will reap the benefits somewhere in year seven or eight and each year after that. However, if you are merely marketing today to get out as quickly as you can tomorrow, then why would you willingly make a larger investment for something that will pay off when you are not even the owner of the property any longer? This answer is simple—value. If you are marketing and selling value, then it benefits you to advertise your external green strategy or the sustainable elements of your project or development. Not only might people buy just because the property is green (a quickly emerging trend) but it will also add value to your immediate costs and financial considerations.

When selling a property or development deal, the capitalization rate is one of the key factors you must evaluate. The capitalization rate assists in determining the cost to operate the property and the basis on whether or not you can get the desired return rate on your investment. Not only how much the deal costs but the appraised value is taken into consideration, and the operating costs. If you are selling a newly developed condo project and all the units happen to have green elements like water restriction devices in bathrooms and kitchens, rainwater catchment systems to irrigate lawns, and heat recovery systems that make use of wasted heat by-product for re-circulation and pre-warming air that is to be heated, then perhaps your project will be less costly to operate.

If you can strategically design water saving techniques and incorporate energy-efficient features into your condo, it could be more attractive to and stimulate interest amongst buyers who are connected to sustainability. This is a huge market of folks you can instantly speak to by developing and practicing your external green strategy. Whether they are interested because of existing health concerns (for example, a need for cleaner air intake in lieu of outside air) or they just want to contribute to reducing the harmful effects of the traditional building process, you can market directly to this segment of the population for immediate success and differentiation.

Each developer that aims to get out as quickly as they can creates a project that uses less energy, water and resources to operate and can quickly become a better investment than a traditional deal for the end user, not to mention the perks of being associated with a sustainable development.

If you don't think people are willing to spend extra money for earth-saving amenities, you only need to study development in Battery Park City, New York. This community in lower Manhattan has engaged itself around sustainability and has developed building standards and codes that require any builder with a project in that area to comply. The residents enjoy expansive parks, rooftop gardens, passive solar energy systems, and water reduction and energy conservation measures in the heart of lower Manhattan, and they don't seem to mind paying extra for those amenities.

I often say you only make money in business by doing a few things: 1) selling more stuff, 2) paying less for the stuff you sell, 3) **reducing the cost to operate where you sell your stuff,** 4) changing the laws (lobbying) so you can sell more stuff! By creating a compelling green strategy that focuses on reducing the cost to operate, you have an opportunity to conserve natural resources and pay less for utilities. You also get a chance to score a victory here and create some savings, allowing you to cash in on how effectively you manage your business. These efforts, combined with your environmental focus and social responsibility, support the principles of sustainability and quickly become part of your external strategy and marketing campaign as an active participant in the green revolution!

CHAPTER 12 - BOLD MOVES TO MAKE NOW!

* Understand the green revolution to prevent a barrier to entry similar to the digital divide.

* Follow legislation for new business models that require sustainability, energy efficiency and regulatory compliance.

* Maintain your advantage and be an early adopter of emerging technology before it becomes the law.

* Utilize an external and internal green strategy to not only promote your social responsibility to clients but to also lower your operating costs.

* Promote your environmental consciousness as a differentiator from competitors.

* Evolve your business practices and operations to complement and sustain the built environment.

CHAPTER 13

BE ABOUT PRACTICE

Practice Is Necessary

I am an avid sports fan and often use sports analogies to make a point. I watch a lot of sports on television and even more sports news programming. In this age of YouTube videos and open mic comments, sound bites can create major news exposure and even a cult following. Do you remember the historic playoffs rant when, after losing yet another game, the infamous coach was asked about his team's chances of making the playoffs? He was baffled that someone would even pose the question. He thought they played so badly they had no chance of moving to the playoffs. Sports enthusiasts are familiar with this play on words and several news media outlets have lampooned the term and phrase, making it very memorable and extremely funny. Another one of my favorite moments in sports is not a game-winning touchdown or an "in your face" slam dunk but a few evenly spaced words forging another sound bite, which will be appropriately discussed in this chapter.

At a post-game press conference in 2002, after a vicious media battle with his head coach over his attitude about putting forth effort and missing multiple practices, a well-known athlete spoke the famous words, "We talking about practice, man." He ranted for about three minutes and actually said the word practice 24 times. He was dumbfounded that such a huge amount of energy was being focused on his efforts in practice and not during the games, which he thought mattered most. He felt, *If I can come out and play hurt during the game and still score 30 points or more, why are we so interested in what I do in practice?* "It's just practice, man!" Over and over he exclaimed, "We're just talking about practice." He couldn't understand how or why the attention was focused on his practice regimen or lack thereof.

While I wasn't exactly looking for a metaphor for entrepreneurs to make my point, this issue of adequate practice fits well. While this professional athlete is one of my favorites, I didn't understand how he could be advocating *against* practice. How could he be saying we have more important things to talk about?

At the top of his game, this player averaged Hall of Fame performance numbers in several categories during his 14-year career. As a professional, he was paid millions of dollars to be the best at what he did. It made sense that, in order to be the best, he would also have to practice. But in the press conference, he was asking us not to worry about him missing practice due to injuries, and to just watch him play. Early in his career, I'm sure he practiced for years and years to develop his talent. But it seemed that, at some point, the premium we put on practice started to lose its significance to him. I'm not sure what contributed to his descent from superstar status—perhaps it had something to do with his casual attitude toward practice that had been captured in the press conference.

Unfortunately, many business owners have the same casual attitude about practice and about their firms. They may not be on display at post-game press conferences, but the folks who don't practice speak loud and clear in terms of business growth or its lack thereof.

You must practice to improve your timing, skill and perspective, but most entrepreneurs don't spend a lot of time practicing their craft. When I started playing golf, I was told that I had to play or practice at least two times a week or I would have no chance of getting any better. How many of us can attest to that work ethic? After playing golf for almost seven years, I didn't start to improve until I committed to playing at least once a week during the summer. That still hasn't been enough but I do feel myself getting better each time out. When I play with people who are much better than me, I always ask about their work ethic and practice regimen.

A fellow entrepreneur I know said he played every day, rain or shine. He had a professional golf game and I seriously think he may be auditioning for the pro golfers' tour any day now. He was an artist who ran his business for over 20 years and liked the freedom entrepreneurship offered. He played golf every day and painted all night and proved to me that, as an entrepreneur, if you can't control your time and exercise some freedom, then what are you doing it for? I quickly committed to playing regularly and saw immediate improvement in my game and mental focus.

We all like to get right to it and play the game without spending the countless hours doing our research, perfecting our pitch, or preparing our plans to improve our chances for success. I do agree that once you have the vision for a product, service, or experience, you should get to market as quickly as you can, but that doesn't mean you should forgo your preparation or practice.

If you've ever played team sports, you know the value of practice. I never liked practice but played football throughout high school as an all-state defensive tackle, and during my freshman year in 1985 on the CIAA Championship Hampton University Pirates football team. Whether our team won the championship or finished in last place, we still had to practice every day. We even practiced at double sessions in late August and I really hated that. We practiced from about 10:00 a.m. to 12:30 p.m. and again from 3:00 p.m. to 5:30 p.m. for about four weeks straight. I couldn't always see why it mattered but, after the fact, I realized that each day you practiced, your focus got sharper and you actually got better.

The long hours of practice were essential to getting in shape, learning plays, building a winning spirit and increasing your athletic performance—all in an effort to win on game day. Even if you don't think it matters, they say you play like you practice. When you practice with a winning attitude, things tend to go well for you during the game. When you are sloppy and just go through the motions with no enthusiasm, usually you get creamed on game day. It happens the same way in business.

Teams change every year and only play about 18 games a season, including pre-season (practice games for the games). So why is it that they devote so much time to practice? In a pro football season that lasts from July to January, there are typically 16 regular season games being played. But the teams practice around three hours a day for about six months—during the season, again during the off-season and again in the spring, all in preparation for winning once the season starts.

Why should you, as a business owner, be any different? Can you count the number of hours you logged this year, this month, or this week practicing your business? Do you just get out there and start selling and hope for the best, or are you preparing to improve your focus, your timing and your performance with the client? Whether you are reading three to five newspapers a day, 12 to 18 books a year, or attending four to five conferences per year, you should be able to put a total on your hours of practice. If you cannot do that, you should revise your plan and start working toward a set number of practice hours each week, month, and/or year.

Don't you want to get better? Don't you have to beat the competition? Won't the strongest firms win? Won't the weakest firms drop out? Where will you and your firm be? After a short stint, will you descend from the ranks of success because you couldn't sustain the winning practice attitude you needed to compete at high levels? Will you call a press conference and ask us to overlook your lack of focus, practice and attention to detail and instead hype up your previous accomplishments? When you are prepared and practicing your craft, *making bold moves* is easier and you can make them stick.

Practice to Improve Your Vision and Focus

Daily practice helps to increase timing and focus and also your vision. Have you ever had an experience where you are working in the details of a project and you can't see what is obvious to someone who comes along perhaps only once a month? Building your vision and focus through steady practice can become part of your strategic advantage. Once you are well-tuned to your work and you start exploring your business from all angles, you will be pleasantly surprised at how your vision will become clearer.

In 1997 I worked as a construction project manager in the field, building a new $50 million school (from the ground up) in the Bronx. I was tasked with many things but my primary focus was managing the day-to-day operations of the general contractor and its subcontractors, and monitoring daily activities involving architectural, mechanical and structural engineers, and specialty lab inspection personnel. We often received inspections from safety personnel and quality control engineers, which I was usually prepared for even though it was their job to find things that I couldn't see.

The thing that bothered me the most was when my boss would visit the site, which was only about once a quarter. He would always manage to point out little things that I had not noticed. Although he was a technical guy and definitely knew how to build, I always thought that, because I was there every day, I knew more about the project than anyone else ever could. I probably did but that doesn't mean I didn't miss the routine issue on occasion. This further confirmed that, because my boss was used to looking at many projects from a very high level, he chose only to focus on a few things. He was also practicing every day but being consumed by the details of many projects across the agency taught him to quickly pick out the most pressing details that mattered in his evaluations. This differed greatly from my job, which required me to hold almost all of the details about everything happening at the new school.

I did practice every day but only saw the details that were in front of me. By practicing at a higher level and consuming more data, reports and research, and making field visits, my boss was practicing at a rate much greater than mine, which ultimately improved his focus. He was able to see greater detail and critical activity in an instant, without having to be on site each day. Once your focus has improved and the rate of your decision making accelerates, you will find that your perspective becomes clearer and you are prepared to perform at a higher capacity than before.

Athletes practice to improve their performance, timing and skills and business professionals should be doing the same. You will find that your performance in front of the client on "game day," when it matters most, will be that much better.

Practice in Business Applications

On the business level, practice will come in all forms. As you focus on increased practice methods, you will find all sorts of opportunities to prepare yourself for growth and success. Whether attending conferences or sitting in on monthly gatherings of business owners like yourself, a regular and consistent effort to work on your craft is necessary to build your business. Once you start to look for ways to better prepare yourself and your product, service, or experience, you will be amazed to find that applications to help you do that are all over the place.

Now that you are starting to assess the various applications to better prepare your business, you will need to develop a strict, daily practice regimen to make what you learn stick and further your dreams. The word regimen is loosely defined as a regulated course or manner of living intended to preserve or restore health or attain some result. For our purposes, do me a favor and replace health with wealth—they are actually interchangeable to me—and read along with the definition I use: *A regimen is a regulated course or manner of living intended to preserve or restore wealth.* Does that sound better? Now ask yourself, *what does my practice regimen consist of?* How many hours per day or week am I devoting to practicing my business? You might not like the answer but, whatever it is, resolve to do better by using these suggestions.

Software Utilization

You might find that the best applications for practicing your business are software related. How many of us actually know how to use our software to its fullest capacity? While the statement *"We only use about 10% of our brains"* can be argued as myth or fact, the reality is we are probably not getting all we can out of ourselves. It is the same with your business software.

Are you harnessing the capability of the bells and whistles you purchased in that premium version of software or are you using it for the most basic tasks only? Practice using it, allow the applications to assist you in further developing your resources and benefit from it. By increasing your software aptitude and capacity, you will improve your use and functionality. Make it your business to commit to a practice regimen that includes technology efficiency across the platforms you regularly use. Use the tutorials, take additional classes, buy customized training and think about sitting in on a certification class for a software application. It doesn't mean you will start a career as a programmer, but you will probably understand more of how to do what you want to do, with ease.

Read, Read, Read

While romance novels may be your thing, I'm asking you to consider another genre of books—business books. I'm talking about how-to books, biographies, motivational and technical books. This type of practice allows you to learn not only from the material but also from the mistakes and successes of others. I spend a lot of time reading business biographies because they give me a different perspective on achieving my goals and my general approach to business. From Sean "Diddy" Combs, Sam Walton, Barack Obama, Mike Bloomberg, Magic Johnson, Madame C.J. Walker, and T. Boone Pickens to R. Donahue Peebles, Donald Trump, Richard Branson, Russell Simmons, Isadore Sharp and Ben & Jerry, each story not only clues me in to their struggle and success but it strengthens my spirit to see that they all overcame various obstacles to meet their success. And I can, too. There are lots of common threads across successful peoples' lives and seeing how they made it and where they went wrong sheds some light on where I want to direct my path.

Although my schedule is hectic, I usually read anywhere from 16 to 20 books a year. According to an Associated Press poll, about 25% of Americans have not read a book in the last year. Moreover, only about one-third of Americans read at least 10 books last year. So how do we get an advantage and use this information to our benefit? Well, you are competing with those same Americans who are not reading and that may not be a bad thing for you. If one in four Americans is not reading at all and only one in three Americans read at least 10 books, what kind of advantage do you think you could gain over most Americans? Furthermore, even fewer Americans actually own businesses. According to a 2004 statistics report, only 11% of Americans were business owners. Even though that statistic may have been updated with the 2010 Census, I'm willing to bet that we are not yet at the point where one in three or one in four (25% - 33%) Americans are business owners.

This means you are working against a bunch of unprepared competitors. So crush them. I'm not sure how you feel, but I would feel great about having such a huge advantage if I knew I read more and practiced

MAKE A BOLD MOVE

Commit to reading two to three business books a month for a tremendous competitive advantage over your competitors. Remember, the average American, who you might be competing against, only reads one to two books a year. Imagine how better informed your perspective will be due to lessons learned from others' mistakes and victories.

133

more than others. Your business needs every advantage to win, so add an aggressive reading schedule to your practice regimen as well. You will find a list of some of my favorite books at the end of this book for your review and practice. Hopefully, you can get something out of them and, perhaps, get even more out of them than I did.

Internet Research & Blogs

There is a plethora of information available, and only when you focus on practice will that information appear in your vision. It may seem confusing to start or get help on your business at first, but there are so many sources of free information available on the Internet that you should have access to whatever you need. Time is required to do the research and navigate the opportunities but, if you are practicing your business in order to increase your timing, skill and performance, you will find help readily available. Whether you are viewing your favorite web-based small business resource center for answers to pressing questions and statistical data or tuning in to a popular video blog, make use of expert advice on the web. That is not to say that all information on the web is credible, but you would be surprised at what you can get from popular, well-known individuals and self-described experts alike.

Our firm operates a video blog titled *Making Bold Moves*, mainly for the emerging entrepreneur or person interested in getting started. We believe that anyone who is thinking of quitting their job to start a business or risking their retirement savings to fund their dream or considering greatly modifying their family life and schedule is definitely a candidate for watching our weekly show. Sometimes you need a bit more motivation to understand that someone else's path may not be that different from yours—and, yes, you can do it, too. We are not focused on selling on the web but working to build a community of trust, where people know they can get inspiration and credible information from a reliable, well-experienced source. It really is not rocket science. If you can share what you have learned from your experiences and have had some good experiences, then you can provide some value to someone else.

I am also starting a blog with my wife on BlogTalkRadio that discusses success in business and marriage called *Business Bliss and Marital Success* where we discuss lessons learned by running separate, successful business ventures for over 10 years, all while supporting a healthy family and marriage of over 17 years. You can't do much in business without a willing partner or spouse and there is a lot that goes into building that kind of support for one another and each other's businesses. Together, we've done a lot, seen even more and have a lot to share. For those of you who are ready and willing to practice your business, *make a bold move* and listen in on our weekly show. Continue your practice by using informative web resources and data centers—along with active participation in forums, blogs and similar interest groups—to continually sharpen your business perspective.

Cross-Conference Attendance

Attending industry conferences is a great way to practice your business and sharpen your skills. Cutting-edge technology and new developments are presented at annual conferences and that provides an opportunity for you to not only learn but to also dialogue with professionals in your industry on the latest issues. This keeps you current and can contribute to shaping your perspective through data and common research.

Strategically moving out of your comfort zone for cross-conference attendance opportunities can solidify your current knowledge and expand limited expertise areas. Imagine if you could take your knowledge and cross pollinate with others in industries related to yours that are perhaps on the fringe. This would allow you to develop new customers and target them for market purposes, but it would also expand your knowledge and perspective from a different angle. The networking and relationship building would be valuable and you may find that what is common knowledge in your industry might make you an expert in other circles.

If you are a technology professional, you probably would gain a lot from attending conferences on emerging technology and new developments in your specific field of study. But what if you attended a law enforcement conference and had an opportunity to deliver your so-called "common knowledge" to a group of leading police directors who purchase technology? While you won't know all there is to know about policing communities in the 21st century, you may very well be a new knowledge base on how technology is solving problems in that area. Certainly, if you are not the featured speaker, you can at least attend the conference and learn the pressing issues facing that industry in an effort to create the "killer app" that solves their problems. Either way you are actively practicing your business and learning about new development, and in this case, doing market research on a new line of potential business. No matter how you look at it, it works. You win and have improved your performance for the next time you are in front of your clients.

Seminars and Professional Development Classes

In the myriad ways to practice your business, don't leave out your own professional development. When was the last time you attended a class to get an edge? Just like licensed professionals are required to take annual credit-hour classes to maintain their licensing, you should be doing the same. While professional examination boards regulate these requirements for architects, engineers and energy/sustainability professionals (LEED APs—Leadership in Energy and Environmental Design Accredited Professionals), you, as the business owner, should be in charge of regulating and updating your credentials for business.

Would you be a better business person if you were required to take at least 15 to 20 credit hours of courses each year to stay in business? I think it would be a tremendous advantage and contribute to your success. It would probably reduce the failure rate of start-up businesses, as well. What most people do is just like passing a driver's test and obtaining a license. Once you receive the license you aren't even thinking about taking another class, only getting out on the road. I will agree that the more you drive, the better driver you will become because driving is a form of practice, but what about when your skills atrophy, or your timing is off, or you have had an accident or two? Should you be required to pass another test? Won't you be required to take a defensive driving course to reinstate your license if you have too many moving violations? Why is it that we don't have a requirement like this for entrepreneurs? If you are racking up catastrophes and capital losses, perhaps you should be required to go back to class until you get it right. But that doesn't usually happen.

Our firm leads a successful contractor training and development program for a public agency in New York City. When contractors fall down on the job or continually make the same mistakes, they are required to attend classes for correction. Furthermore, they are often suspended from bid opportunities until they have confirmed that they have taken mandatory classes and made some improvement where they were struggling. This makes a lot of sense but needs to be more regulated by individuals in business.

As part of your practice regimen, you need to determine how you will manage and update your credentials each year. You should be seeking out classes and seminars to attend to increase your capacity and skill. Timing is everything and if yours is off your business may fail. Don't run the risk of failing just because you were not interested in practice. Remember that your regimen is your course of action or manner of living intended to preserve or restore wealth. Maintain your education, skill, timing and performance, and don't be like the superstar athlete who exclaimed, *"It's just practice man!"*

CHAPTER 13 - BOLD MOVES TO MAKE NOW!

* Practice is necessary, so make it part of your regular business process.

* Improve your timing, skill and perspective through a constant regimen of regular repetition.

* Log the hours you spend preparing to be a better business owner on a yearly, monthly and weekly basis.

* Accelerate your decision making process by improving your focus and data collection.

* Take the time to learn technology applications to capitalize on more of their hidden value.

* Read two to three books a month on business or technical-related matters.

* Harness the power of the Internet for research as opposed to just browsing.

CHAPTER 14

WHAT DO WE DO NEXT?

Develop the Plan, Assemble the Team and Get Mentored!

We have now gone over several concepts you are required to consider if you want to grow to the next level, but we still need to manage that effort. Although it is easy to review the actions and techniques we discussed, *making bold moves* will demand focus to see those moves through and a team of internal and external resources to get you to the next level. The framework has been established to quickly ramp up your firm and grow revenues to multimillion-dollar levels in about 500 days from the time you make the commitment and deliver the passion, discipline and focus necessary to achieve your goals. However, nothing works without a thoughtful and targeted plan.

Develop the Plan

While the information in this book is still fresh, take the opportunity to devise a plan for how you will take action over the next several months. The plan should include not only a list of actions and potential outcomes but also a timeline and schedule so you can track your progress. You should also include a vision board of what your success will look like once you achieve your desired goals. If you plan on making enough money to move your venture to a tropical locale where, perhaps, you play golf twice a week, find a picture of the locale and post it on your vision board along with several crucial milestones you will mark in achieving that goal. This has the potential to improve your focus and serve as a motivating factor when your present working conditions and success are not yet consistent with where you ultimately want to be.

The timeline and schedule will allow you to create the right expectations for how and when you should be taking action and, presumably, how soon you should expect to see progress. The timeline will also identify what major events/activities would typically occur over the next 500-day period and what actions are required to make those events/activities happen. If you expect to exhibit your product at a trade show that occurs eight months from now, thoughtfully jot down what steps you'll need to take and when they should be completed to make sure you are on track. Similarly, if you plan on leaving your day job to pursue your venture full-time, your timeline should include extraction details including what activities would lead to you ultimately walking out on your boss 12 to 18 months from now. As I stated in Chapter 1, leaving my job in 2005 included securing minority business certifications, which are not obtained overnight. This process can take up to nine months and is also contingent on tax documents that would have been prepared one to two years prior. However you do it, you must plan the process up front in order to create the conditions that will fulfill your expectations.

Reviewing this type of milestone timeline regularly will reinforce what you should be doing and serve as a not so subtle reminder, especially when you attach action dates to each item. Now you can measure what you *are* doing against what you *should be* doing and preparing for. You can also better plan and project future events and your readiness to enter specific markets based on your strictly followed schedule and regimen.

This action plan will not only consist of things you need to do but will include the people you need in order to get it done— folks inside your organization and, in some cases, folks outside of your organization. Simply put, consider your inner team to be your company staff, which will play a huge role in preparing you for the next opportunity. You must value the contribution and thought process of the people who are in the trenches with you and closest to your work and, in some cases, your clients. As long as you select them well and train them right, they will usually have a good perspective on what it takes to succeed for your clients and how to maintain a winning rapport with customers. Each and every chance you get to develop a more informed perspective of your firm, talk to your staff, evaluate what they have to say, then formulate a new opinion.

Assemble the Team

Early on, my experience made me feel like I could only trust folks in my business whom I had known for over 20 years. But it seemed unlikely that I would be able to successfully build an organization on those terms. Initially, I thought I would have to

140

delegate trust to new hires who had the skills we desperately needed but who, nonetheless, were folks I might have been meeting for the first time. While having to do that is inevitable, you can still rely on long lasting relationships where trust has already been cultivated to help build your organization from within. While I am quick to say, "The firm will only grow on the efforts of folks much smarter than me," I am aware of the effort required to find smart people, inside or outside of my comfort network, and I do still value loyalty and familiarity.

I can say that our firm has grown because of at least two very successful relationships I have held for over 20 years. Our current Vice President, Ceylon Frett, has been a tremendous asset and our relationship has flourished over the last 25 years. We have developed a trust and a confidence where we can share ideas and criticize each others' actions without any harm done. We have also gained a mutual respect for the way each of us can charge ahead in aggressively pursuing the company's stated goals. We know each others' strengths and weaknesses and can adequately support the company's vision through our actions.

Another key staffer who has proven successful in building our firm is Johnnie Harris, Director of Client Services. Johnnie and I have worked together for about 21 years in different capacities. I actually worked for him on an early assignment where he was an agency executive who exhibited true character and always advocated for parity and equality amongst the firms he managed. His expertise is extensive and his opinion is highly regarded, which makes him extremely valuable to our firm and our clients. Johnnie also operates on a calm, reserved level that creates a nice balance to the pace at which I often work.

Spend time assembling the right team and making sure that the folks you select are strategically appropriate to your environment and also have the skills, motivation and knowledge required to advance your firm in your market. Of course, you will still need to provide some organizational effort to support the teams, including incentives for high performance and a clear understanding of your expectations for their work. If you succeed here, you can build and sustain a performance culture within your firm that will attract talent and generate revenues required for your immediate growth.

Continue to assemble a winning team and manage the pieces for strategic fit. Don't be afraid to tinker with the process and perhaps change the lineup as new demands are put on your business. Folks you worked with in the start-up stages will not always fit in with future plans as you grow, so be prepared to make and live with some hard decisions about their continued employment with the firm.

Get Mentored!

No matter how good you are, you won't be able to do it alone. So if at all possible, seek mentoring at every opportunity. Everyone knows the value of having a good professional team, which includes attorneys, accountants, bankers and insurance brokers, but do not underestimate the value of a professional mentor—someone who has accomplished more than you have in business—whether they're in your industry or not.

I have seen, through my firm's growth, how experienced and seasoned mentors can affect you, personally, and your business. I have had the pleasure of a couple of formal and some not so formal mentoring relationships with wise industry professionals who blazed trails long before I began my journey. In some cases, my mentors have operated within my market, allowing me the opportunity to team up with them and pursue contracting opportunities. In other cases, they have operated outside of my environment but still in intense business sectors that have fueled my growth. These local sages usually have seen and done a lot of what you may be trying to do and can assist you in your development if you are willing to learn from them. The balance is perfect since they have the expertise and usually want to impart knowledge to younger emerging businesses.

I have been fortunate to have a great team of mentors who I can call on in different situations. I consider them my unofficial board of directors because I can count on their varying degrees of assistance and wisdom regarding key issues related to my growth and their feedback has assisted me in operating my firm.

One of my mentors has operated in my market sector for over 20 years and has now transitioned his firm's services to development. His expertise in managing all issues associated with developing an organization with annual revenues of $50 million have proved invaluable. I have learned how to better negotiate, build and utilize political capital, as well as maintain a respectful demeanor in building a consortium of support in the industry.

Another of my mentors was responsible for advocating, through the legal system, for minority business participation on federally funded contracts as early as 1968. He was then executing what are now referred to as community benefits agreements—economic and financial considerations for community partners that are affected by infrastructure projects—for some of the largest public project expansions in the New York/New Jersey market, including Newark Liberty Airport and the University of Medicine and Dentistry in Newark. I have learned many lessons through countless stories he has shared with me from his many years of fighting for minority business legislation and contracts. His work has afforded him tremendous influence among community stakeholders in a very strong regional market and I am glad to have his confidence.

Yet another of my mentors founded a five-branch community bank in New Jersey that provides business financing to reputable firms, including yours truly! He has counseled me on finance operations, as well as on staffing and human resources issues, which has allowed my firm to grow our revenue and staff by at least 30% each year in our initial years of operation.

Still another of my formal mentor relationships has resulted in me having access to the CEO of a $200 million professional services firm engaged in government contracting and several state and municipal vertical markets. Through this relationship, I have been counseled on employee relations, handling employee turnover and given strategies for managing tough business and economic challenges presented by this recession. I give major credit to and have derived extreme value from my mentors—on business issues as well as political strategy—as I continue to plan and execute daily operations for the firm.

We all have heard the saying, *Let's not re-create the wheel*. But for a lot of entrepreneurs who have to trust themselves and work alone to get their ideas off the ground, the concept of "re-creating the wheel" happens countless times in early stage firms. There is really no need to make the same mistakes twice, so be diligent, seek counsel in mentors and categorize your learning, as well as theirs, so you can recall the knowledge required for the growth goals you will ultimately attain.

Conclusions

You now have the tools, resources, staff and this book as a guide to assist you on your way. I trust that you will or have already supplied the good ideas to get started, along with a value proposition for a much-needed product, service or experience with market differentiation that will sustain your competitive advantage against your peers. It's time to test the concepts attached as well as your willingness and passion for creating the business success you have dreamed of.

To further complement what we have discussed through my journey, I have also prepared a suggested reading list of 54 of my favorite books, which have afforded me knowledge through others' journeys. The books are either business texts, business biographies, or biographies about people I believe had a tremendous effect on their industry or market. I do expect that you will preview the list, then read the books, build your own conclusions and learn even more lessons than I did, from these stories and others, too.

Once you get to the list you will see why there are 54 books on it. Yes I have created a bit more work for you to do on your own that will get you to your goals. Remember, I am here for you, and the list of 54 books in Appendix 54 indicates the level of commitment required to practice your craft and set your mind right.

In order for you to start *making bold moves,* you will need to be very comfortable with taking calculated risks and responding to challenges. You made a great decision in buying this book and committing the time required to finish it but the journey can't end there. Learn from my story and apply the lessons discussed in each chapter as you plan and take action, but also accept this challenge to execute a couple of more things on your own:

✓ *Pledge to develop and implement a winning plan for success over the next 500 days!*

✓ *Pledge to build a multimillion-dollar business within the next 500 days!*

✓ *Pledge to use the lessons in this book to track your progress over the next 500 days!*

✓ *Pledge to guarantee result-oriented action by delivering your passion over the next 500 days!*

✓ *Pledge to avoid a herd mentality and pursue your goals with vigor over the next 500 days!*

✓ *Pledge to maintain a healthy balance of family, work and play over the next 500 days!*

✓ *Pledge to be faithful and seek that God's will be done for you over the next 500 days!*

Just deciding that you wanted to create multimillion-dollar success in 500 days or less was bold enough. Now I'm more confident than before that your personal commitment, your pledge, your new knowledge from my story and the lessons you will learn from others will give you all you need to be *making bold moves* and achieving the goals you desire! Continue to push for it to happen! Be determined to have it happen! Be prepared to see it happen! Now do the work required to make it happen! I hope to see your journey, progress, challenges and success stories as you post them at ***makingboldmovesnow.com***.

It's time to respond to the challenge and come to the stage *now*! You've decided you want to win and have planned for your success. You have evaluated risks associated with your venture and made accommodations for the potential rewards. You have learned how to create wins for the client and how to sell services to larger prime consultants and clients. What's even better is you have learned how to land the "big fish" client and understand how political strategy can assist you in keeping them. You have figured out how to get paid now while you are waiting for your bright ideas to bear fruit and have learned the value in community service. You have seen how creating a social media strategy can promote your business and have also learned how developing a green strategy can cause differentiation. Now that you are ready to put your plan in action and really be about practice, you know what to do next. Immediately implement this template for *Creating Multimillion-Dollar Success in 500 Days or Less* as your blueprint for *Making Bold Moves!*

CHAPTER 14 - BOLD MOVES TO MAKE NOW!

❋ Dream big and be ready to take the steps required to move now, and document your progress.

❋ Devise your execution plan and create a vision board for success.

❋ Take extreme care in assembling a winning team and constantly evaluate the need to shuffle resources as necessary.

❋ Get comfortable with risk taking to increase your business offerings, expertise and proficiency.

❋ Read this book more than once to commit the concepts to memory, and regularly practice getting better.

❋ Pass this book along or buy another copy for someone who you know needs this type of fuel to get started.

❋ Stay connected to the resources you trust that supply you with the information you need on your journey to success.

❋ Blog with us about your progress at www.makingboldmovesnow.com.

❋ Create your own version of success in 500 days or less!

Appendix 54

RECOMMENDED READING

I have listed 54 of my favorite books as suggested reading. Why 54? Simple—three books per month for a consecutive 18 months will get you to the target of 54 books over the course of 500 days. If you will be *making bold moves* you must make time for reading, no matter how busy you think you are or how full your daily schedule actually is. Achieving multimillion-dollar success will require that you read at least two to three books per month, but I prefer that you read three. If I did it, you can do it too.

Choose from these 54 to last you the next 18 months or so. I hope you enjoy them as much as I did. The books are not necessarily ranked in order of preference but rather as they came to mind—although favorites sometimes have a way of creeping into your consciousness first.

1. *Why Should White Guys Have All the Fun?:* How Reginald Lewis Created a Billion-Dollar Business Empire by Reginald F. Lewis and Blair S. Walker

2. *Rich Dad, Poor Dad:* What the Rich Teach Their Kids About Money—That the Poor and the Middle Class Do Not! (Miniature Edition) by Robert T. Kiyosaki

3. *Black Titan:* A.G. Gaston and the Making of a Black American Millionaire by Carol Jenkins and Elizabeth Gardner Hines

4. *Blue Ocean Strategy:* How to Create Uncontested Market Space and Make Competition Irrelevant by W. Chan Kim and Renee Mauborgne

5. *Barack, Inc.:* Winning Business Lessons of the Obama Campaign by Barry Libert and Rick Faulk

6. *Delivering Happiness:* A Path to Profits, Passion, and Purpose by Tony Hsieh

7. *The Wal-Mart Way:* The Inside Story of the Success of the World's Largest Company by Don Soderquist

8. *How to Succeed in Business Without Being White:* Straight Talk on Making It in America by Earl G. Graves

9. *Rich Dad's Conspiracy of the Rich:* The 8 New Rules of Money by Robert T. Kiyosaki

10. *How The Mighty Fall:* And Why Some Companies Never Give In by Jim Collins

11. *The First Billion Is the Hardest:* Reflections on a Life of Comebacks and America's Energy Future by T. Boone Pickens

12. *ESPN The Company:* The Story and Lessons Behind the Most Fanatical Brand in Sports by Anthony F. Smith and Keith Hollihan

13. *On Her Own Ground:* The Life and Times of Madam C.J. Walker (Lisa Drew Books) by A'Lelia Bundles

14. *The Real Pepsi Challenge:* How One Pioneering Company Broke Color Barriers in 1940s American Business by Stephanie Capparell

15. *The Smartest Guys in the Room:* The Amazing Rise and Scandalous Fall of Enron by Bethany McLean and Peter Elkind

16. *Crush It!:* Why NOW Is the Time to Cash In on Your Passion by Gary Vaynerchuk

17. *Black Enterprise Titans of The B.E. 100s:* Black CEOs Who Redefined and Conquered American Business (Black Enterprise Books) by Derek T. Dingle

18. *Powerhouse Principles:* The Ultimate Blueprint for Real Estate Success in an Ever-Changing Market by Jorge Perez and Donald J. Trump

19. *Switch:* How to Change Things When Change Is Hard by Chip Heath and Dan Heath

20. *Empire State of Mind:* How Jay-Z Went from Street Corner to Corner Office by Zack O'Malley Greenburg

21. *Winning* by Jack Welch and Suzy Welch

22. *The E-Myth* by Michael E. Gerber

23. *Adam By Adam:* The Autobiography of Adam Clayton Powell, Jr. by Adam Clayton Powell

24. *The Upside of the Downturn:* Ten Management Strategies to Prevail in the Recession and Thrive in the Aftermath by Geoffrey Colvin

25. *Good Is Not Enough:* And Other Unwritten Rules for Minority Professionals by Keith R. Wyche and Sonia Alleyne

26. *The Richest Man in Babylon* by George S. Clason

27. *Stop Acting Rich: ... And Start Living Like A Real Millionaire* by Thomas J. Stanley

28. *Secrets of the Millionaire Mind:* Mastering the Inner Game of Wealth by T. Harv Eker

29. *The Millionaire Next Door:* Surprising Secrets of America's Wealthy by Thomas Stanley and William Danko

30. *The Automatic Millionaire:* A Powerful One-Step Plan to Live and Finish Rich by David Bach

31. *Becoming a Millionaire God's Way:* Getting Money to You, Not from You by C. Thomas Anderson

32. *Do You!:* 12 Laws to Access the Power in You to Achieve Happiness and Success by Russell Simmons and Chris Morrow

33. *Super Rich:* A Guide to Having it All by Russell Simmons and Chris Morrow

34. *32 Ways to Be a Champion in Business* by Earvin Johnson

35. *The Brand Within:* The Power of Branding from Birth to the Boardroom (Display of Power) by Daymond John and James "Jim" Cramer

36. *The 50th Law* by 50 Cent and Robert Greene

37. *Bad Boy:* The Influence of Sean "Puffy" Combs on the Music Industry by Ronin Ro

38. *The 360 Degree Leader:* Developing Your Influence from Anywhere in the Organization by John C. Maxwell

39. *The House the Rockefellers Built:* A Tale of Money, Taste, and Power in Twentieth-Century America (John MacRae Books) by Robert F. Dalzell and Lee Baldwin Dalzell

40. *The Peebles Principles:* Tales and Tactics from an Entrepreneur's Life of Winning Deals, Succeeding in Business, and Creating a Fortune from Scratch by R. Donahue Peebles and J. P. Faber

41. *Aim High:* Common Sense Success for Common Sense People by Herbert K. Ames

42. *Mike Bloomberg:* Money, Power, Politics by Joyce Purnick

43. *Four Seasons:* The Story of a Business Philosophy by Isadore Sharp

44. *The Adventures of Grandmaster Flash:* My Life, My Beats by Grandmaster Flash and David Ritz

45. *The Mary Kay Way:* Timeless Principles from America's Greatest Woman Entrepreneur by Mary Kay Ash

46. *Mind Right, Money Right:* 10 Laws of Financial Freedom by Ash Cash, Amina Phelps, Bellinger Moye and Jason Lalor

47. *From the Trash Man to the Cash Man:* How Anyone Can Get Rich Starting from Anywhere by Myron Golden

48. *Dreaming No Small Dreams:* William R. Harvey's Visionary Leadership by Lois Benjamin

49. *Do the Right Thing:* How Dedicated Employees Create Loyal Customers and Large Profits (paperback) by James F. Parker

50. *Hug Your Customers:* The Proven Way to Personalize Sales and Achieve Astounding Results by Jack Mitchell

51. *The Power Of Less:* The Fine Art Of Limiting Yourself To The Essential ... In Business And In Life by Leo Babauta

52. *Aol.com:* How Steve Case Beat Bill Gates, Nailed the Netheads, and Made Millions in the War for the Web by Kara Swisher

53. *Good to Great:* Why Some Companies Make the Leap ... and Others Don't by Jim Collins

54. *Built to Last:* Successful Habits of Visionary Companies by Jim Collins and Jerry I. Porras

ABOUT THE AUTHOR

William S. Parrish, Jr. LEED AP, BD+C

With over 24 years of experience in construction management, Mr. Parrish has consistently coordinated and delivered large-scale, multi-stage construction projects where success depends on the balance of community stakeholders, civic representation, agency resources and technical staff.

William started NobleStrategy as a one-man consultancy in 2002 while working full time. He quit his day job in 2005, and within a year forged strategic partnerships and won several state agency contracts for construction management, based on his knowledge and relationships.

William's vision and expertise at planning, coordinating and delivering large-scale, multi-stage projects has driven the expansion of NobleStrategy to its position as a top construction resource, focused on delivering estimating, safety analysis, scheduling, contractor mentoring, sustainable design and construction practices and project management to public and private entities in the education, civic and corporate sectors.

A LEED accredited professional since 2004, Mr. Parrish is leading the effort in sustainable construction practices, assisting project owners and teams in a winning approach to managing energy efficient green construction projects and attaining LEED project certification where required.

Mr. Parrish graduated from Hampton University with a Bachelor of Science in Building Construction Technology and completed his Master of Science in Management of Technology at Polytechnic University of N.Y. Mr. Parrish is a NYC Building Department Licensed Site Safety Manager and holds certifications in Zoning & Land Use, Brownfield Redevelopment, Construction Litigation and Wetlands Delineation. Mr. Parrish is also an Adjunct Professor at New York University, Schack Institute of

151

Real Estate, School of Continuing and Professional Studies since 2007 and won the coveted NYU Dr. Martin Luther King Jr. Faculty Award in 2011.

Mr. Parrish is an active board member of the Capital Region Minority Chamber of Commerce, City of Newark Workforce Investment Board and ACE-Mentor-NJ, as well as contributing member of the Construction Management Association of America, the New York and New Jersey Chapters of the United States Green Building Council, the Development School for Youth/All-Stars Program, GrassRoots Foundation and the Eta Pi Chapter of the Omega Psi Phi Fraternity, Inc.

To purchase additional copies of this book please visit our website:

www.makingboldmovesnow.com

"Like" us on facebook.com/makingboldmovesnow

"Follow us" on Twitter.com/makingboldmoves

DISCARD